"*The Father Glorified* grabs our hearts with the stories of common people used of God to spark Disciple Making Movements in difficult places. Surrendered hearts, obedient faith, courageous love . . . such are the marks of those whom God uses to accomplish great things. Cityteam is uniquely qualified to tell their stories and distill principles essential to the discipling of nations."

—**Dr. Dean Carlson**, Vice-President of Global Ministries, OC International

"While many approach evangelism and discipleship by asking God to bless what they are doing, Cityteam is determined to do what God is blessing. Their results are an astounding fruitfulness. The stories and insights in this book will inspire your soul and challenge your methods."

—**Robert Crosby**, Author of *The Teaming Church*, Professor of Practical Theology at Southeastern University

"For sheer excitement and compelling stories, *The Father Glorified* is hard to beat. If you will look closely you will discover the simple principles from God's Word that will help you write stories of your own. Early in ministry, a veteran missionary told me, 'Every now and then Jesus stops and whispers in our ear, '*I'm going this way. Do you want to come*'? He waits for just a moment before he moves on to someone else.' When you read *The Father Glorified*, be ready to hear a whisper."

—**James Forlines**, Executive Director, Final Command Ministries

"I personally know Pat along with the other amazing individuals with Cityteam and have seen the incredible things that God is doing through them. I have traveled the distant dusty roads in Africa with Cityteam and witnessed first-hand the miraculous movement of their work. God is using them in spreading His message in almost epic dimensions along with empowering simple people to be used of God in mighty ways. I encourage you to read this book. It will ignite within you a fresh fire of service to our Lord in ways you could never imagine."

—**Robert Cornuke**, Founder of The BASE Institute,
author of *The Pravda Messenger*, Host of Gutsy
Christianity on the NRB Channel

"Everyone loves a story about justice or redemption. *The Father Glorified* is a book filled with such stories who true-life individuals who met God in the unlikeliest of places, through the most miraculous situations. You are as certain to get chills up your spine as you are to be inspired by the way Jesus is using ordinary people to bring extraordinary transformation in the Muslim world as well as communities in our own backyard."

—**Tim Stevens**, Executive Pastor, Granger Community
Church and author of *Vision: Lost and Found*

"Want to know how Jesus continues to build his church? Read this book to learn how ordinary people, divinely empowered, are building his church in the most unsuspecting places. *The Father Glorified* takes us on a gripping journey through a web of relations of ordinary people being used of God to do extraordinary things. It's a chronicle of real people encountering Jesus and becoming agents of peace and transformation in their communities. The book is not advocating a new "7-step methodology" to successful church planting but instead testifying that faith, dependence and obedience lead to transformation and fruitful multiplication.

I am actively implementing the principles illustrated in these pages and hope you will too! Indeed, may Father be glorified!

—**Rev. John Becker**, Director of Ministries, Africa Inland Mission International

"Pat and Greg give us an incredible glimpse into what God is doing right now through his people around the world. This collection of true accounts reveals the amazing power and work of the Holy Spirit in and through the lives of seemingly unlikely people. Reading these stories gives me great hope in what is possible through God – when we are faithful and simply obey. *The Father Glorified* is a great gift to the body of Christ."

—**Eric Hanson**, *International Impact Director, Christ Community Church & Missions Consultant, Mission Excell*

"In *The Father Glorified*, Pat Robertson and Greg Benoit of Cityteam let us in on some of their incredible, first-hand stories of practical ways God is at work in the world today. Through each story, they share proven principles for Disciple Making Movements for anyone who wants to see God work in similar ways in their own small corner of the world. I encourage you to read this book with the perspective that God can use you too to have an irreplaceable role in the Kingdom."

—**Matt Brown**, Evangelist, Author and Founder of Think Eternity

"Using the most humble, mundane and unlikeliest of people and circumstances, God manifests miracle after miracle in these amazing stories that will encourage and challenge you like modern-day parables. *The Father Glorified* undeniably illustrates

God's power to make strong disciples in unorthodox, mystifying ways—much like the movements Cityteam has been part of. It is powerful and inspiring."

—**Ame Mahler Beanland**, *New York Times* Bestselling co-author of *Nesting* and *Postcards from the Bump*

"*The Father Glorified* reminds us all of the tremendous impact Cityteam is having around the world regardless of the language or culture. This is illustrated by individuals in the book who have reached a point of humility to receive God's grace through our Savior, Isa al Masih."

—**Russell Brown**, Chairman/President (ret.) Harry J. Lloyd Charitable Trust

"The *Father Glorified* is filled with stories that will expand your faith, challenge you to pray big prayers, and start looking for what God is doing and how you can partner with him. I highly recommend this book."

–**Josh Reich**, Founding Pastor, Revolution Church in Tucson

"Jesus taught us to love God, love others, and be a witness for him by telling stories and asking good questions. *Father Glorified* is not only an excellent read about a process that is happening today to meet Jesus' teaching, but it is a great representation of compassionate discipleship that brings Good News to any tribe or nation. You'll be better—and challenged—as a result."

—**Paul Schaller**, Christian entrepreneur and former CEO of Quest Aircraft

THE FATHER GLORIFIED

True Stories of God's Power through Ordinary People

PATRICK ROBERTSON
DAVID WATSON
WITH GREGORY C. BENOIT

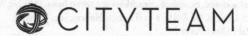

THOMAS NELSON
Since 1798

NASHVILLE   DALLAS   MEXICO CITY   RIO DE JANEIRO

Published in Nashville, Tennessee, by Thomas Nelson. Thomas Nelson is a
registered trademark of Thomas Nelson, Inc.

Pat Robertson's photo taken by Lem Malabuyo

Page design and typesetting by Crosslin Creative

Thomas Nelson, Inc., titles may be purchased in bulk for educational,
business, fund-raising, or sales promotional use. For information, please
e-mail SpecialMarkets@ThomasNelson.com.

Unless otherwise noted, Scripture quotations are taken from THE NEW
KING JAMES VERSION. © 1982 by Thomas Nelson, Inc. Used by
permission. All rights reserved.

All quotations from the Qur'an are from *Qur'an*, tr. Mohammed
Marmaduke Pickthall.

Library of Congress Cataloging-in-Publication Data

9781418547301

Printed in the United States of America

13 14 15 16 17 18 RRD 6 5 4 3 2 1

DEDICATION

From Pat Robertson:

I would like to dedicate this book to David Watson who was willing to be obedient to God and implement the principles God was teaching him, and to freely share them with others.

And to:

The tens of thousands of brave but ordinary men and women whose obedience and faith has been the instrument of the spiritual dynamic of Disciple Making Movements.

CONTENTS

CONTENTS

INTRODUCTION

This book is intended to go hand-in-hand with *Miraculous Movements: How Hundreds of Thousands of Muslims are Falling in Love with Jesus*, by Jerry Trousdale. In that book, Trousdale outlined and explained some of the important principles that are involved in the worldwide Disciple Making Movement, principles that are drawn directly from the teachings of Jesus Christ found in the New Testament. He illustrated those principles with true stories, drawn from hundreds of interviews that he and others have conducted over the last couple of years. This book illustrates those same principles, but with very little didactic comment. Instead, we wanted to let the stories speak for themselves, showing how God is at work around the world today in the lives of millions of ordinary people—not just in the lives of Muslims, not just in Africa, but in the hearts of ordinary people from every background, every tribe, and tongue.

These stories are all true. There are instances where you will meet a character in one chapter who will reappear in a later chapter, and in some of those cases that character is actually a composite of two different people. This was done merely for the sake of the narrative flow within this book; the stories themselves are entirely true, drawn from interviews with the very people who experienced them.

Each chapter will begin with a basic principle of making disciples, citing a Scripture passage from which that principle is drawn. But the stories themselves, as you will see, illustrate many different elements that go into obeying the teachings of Christ on how to go into all the world "and make disciples of all the nations, baptizing them in the name of the Father and of the Son and of the Holy Spirit, teaching them to observe all things that I have commanded you" (Mathew 28:19–20).

We know that these principles work, primarily because Jesus Himself taught them, and secondarily because Cityteam has been implementing them for several years—with dramatic results. We have seen literally hundreds of thousands of ordinary people discovering God through the power of the Holy Spirit and experiencing dramatic transformations in their lives as they begin to study and obey the Word of God. This book, however, is not about statistics; it is about those ordinary people discovering God's truth in every walk of life, from Africa, Nicaragua, the United States, and all over the world. If you would like to learn more, please read *Miraculous Movements* by Jerry Trousdale, or visit our Web site at www.Cityteam.org.

ABOUT THE AUTHORS

Pat Robertson was born in Salt Lake City, Utah, of a French war bride mother and an American GI father. Raised in Columbia, Missouri, Pat joined the US Air Force and spent a tour of duty in Vietnam. Still angry about his parents, divorce and Vietnam, Pat carried that anger into his marriage to Kathy. Their marriage was very turbulent and violent until Pat and Kathy were drawn to Jesus Christ, which saved their marriage. Called to serve God, Pat attended Prairie Bible College where they met the son of the founder of the San Jose Rescue Mission who convinced the young couple to work at a camp for inner-city youth. In 1972 Pat joined the San Jose Rescue Mission, which later became Cityteam, and served in various positions over the years.

Pat believes that God is using Cityteam to be a small part in fulfilling Matthew 24:14: "And this gospel of the kingdom will be preached in all the world as a witness to all the nations, and then the end will come." It was after reading *Good to Great* by Jim Collins and meeting and becoming best friends with his mentor and fellow kingdom servant David Watson that God revealed from His Word the simple methods that Jesus taught His disciples that caused the good news to spread globally two thousand years ago and today through Disciple Making Movements!

David Watson serves as the Vice President of Global Church Planting with Cityteam, San Jose, CA. His primary responsibility is to catalyze Disciple Making Movements in difficult to reach people groups, cities and countries around the world. The primary methodology used is the training of local leaders in Disciple Making Movements, which includes evangelism and disciple making, church planting, leadership, church planting strategies and church planting movements. God has used the leaders David trained to start over 100,000 churches in the past 15 years, and more than 4 million people have been baptized as a result of God's movement in the areas where trained local workers have devoted themselves to disciple-making.

David has been involved in unreached people work since 1986. He and his wife, Jan, are among the pioneers of the non-residential missionary movement, strategy coordinator methodologies, and the focus on the unreached peoples of the world.

David and Jan were married in 1973. They have two sons, one daughter-in-law, and three grandchildren. They served as

Church Planters and Strategy Coordinators for the International Mission Board of the Southern Baptist Convention from October 1985 to March 1999. They have lived and worked in Hong Kong, Malaysia, South Asia, Singapore, and the United States of America. David has trained people in more than one hundred countries.

In the performance of his duties, David has been responsible for starting two mission agencies that focus on unreached peoples and Church Planting Movements. He has also been involved in starting three companies to provide platforms for missionaries and support for missions.

David's long-term plans are to continue facilitating the development of Disciple Making Movements among the unreached peoples of the world, and mentoring leaders in church planting movement methodologies.

Gregory C. Benoit is a freelance writer and editor who was involved in conducting the many interviews which form the foundation of this book. He traveled to Africa with Cityteam personnel, knowing virtually nothing about the dramatic transformations of ordinary people which the Lord is accomplishing in the world today, and returned home a changed man. His hope is that these stories will have the same effect on those who read them.

ABOUT CITYTEAM

Cityteam's mission is the heartbeat of Jesus' words. Jesus preached many great sermons, but three times He commanded His disciples to obey Him in the Great Commandment and the Great Commission. He commanded His disciples to love God with *all* their heart, mind, and strength and also to love their neighbor as much as they love themselves. Jesus also gave the Great Commission where He instructed His disciples to "go make disciples," and they were to go to the ends of the earth to reach every people group. Cityteam has created a simple diagram to express what we believe Jesus said to all of His followers. This expresses what Cityteam believes and seeks to do everywhere God calls us.

LOVE GOD

LOVE YOUR NEIGHBOR

GO MAKE DISCIPLES WHO OBEY

Cityteam's mission statement calls us to transformation here at home and also around the world. We believe it is a transformation that begins in each individual as they respond to God's love, spreads to the family, and transforms the community.

> *In obedience to Christ, passionately transforming individuals, their families, and communities throughout the world.*

Since 1957 Cityteam has provided for the physical, emotional, and spiritual needs of millions of people in San Jose, Oakland, and San Francisco, California; Portland, Oregon; and Chester, Pennsylvania.

Through the years, God has transformed the lives of individuals—as well as their families and communities—who are suffering from poverty, homelessness, and addiction. Besides providing compassion ministries, God has led Cityteam to also focus on making obedient and reproducing disciples of Jesus Christ. By God's remarkable grace, a simple rescue mission that was willing to listen and obey God's instructions is training, equipping, coaching, and mentoring thousands of leaders in hundreds of ministries, serving unreached peoples worldwide.

Cityteam is especially focused in the "10/40 window"—that part of the world where the majority of people are living and dying without a chance to respond to the good news of God's love. A large majority of these families are the poorest of the world's poor!

God has given Cityteam a heart for everyone, everywhere. Through investors, thousands of volunteers, and a small dedicated staff, God has blessed Cityteam to plant more than eighteen thousand churches in North America and around the world, with 584,000 new believers—and still growing. Approximately 41 percent of those are Muslims who found the answers to their prayers in Jesus the Messiah.

GOD'S VISION FOR YOU

If God touched your heart through reading this book and you want to let God use you, then consider partnering with Cityteam. It is God, not us, who speaks to your heart and calls you to become His faithful and fruitful disciples. We are all called to pray, to listen to His Word, to obey Him, and to invest our lives strategically among those who are lost in sin without knowing the God who loves them.

Pray with us that God will speak to more and more people living in darkness through visions and dreams and that they will be drawn to discover and obey God. Pray that the disciple-making teams will find the people of peace that God is calling them to disciple. Pray also for their safety, as they minister in high-risk and sometimes hostile areas. Consider investing with Cityteam, so that you can be a part of seeing hundreds of thousands of new Christ followers becoming trained, equipped, coached, and mentored to disciple the millions of people who have never heard the gospel even once.

If God is calling you to be a part of His miraculous movement in your community, please visit our Cityteam website (www.Cityteam.org) to tell us your personal story, to review our resource materials, or to find a schedule of trainings around the world. You can also e-mail Cityteam at info@cityteam.org.

Our Cityteam staff and prayer partners want to pray for you. If you are planting a church or discipling a community, please visit our Web site at www.cityteam.org/idisciple.

Remember that God chooses to use ordinary people to do extraordinary things. May God also do in you that which is "exceedingly, abundantly beyond all you can ask or even imagine"—He loves you that much!

1

PRAYER

And whatever things you ask in prayer,
believing, you will receive. (Matthew 21:22)

In a mysterious way, prayer moves the hand of God.
When we join together in agreement, praying and
seeking the Lord and His will, He will act in power. As
our story opens, a desperate father prays for his son, and
two elderly women walk into the local police station
to pray—with miraculous results. Prayer is absolutely
the essence of these mighty movements of God! When
we trace backward, we find that someone prayed—
sometimes for an extended time—and God heard and
answered those prayers. The work of God always begins
with and is sustained through prayer, and it is fitting
that our story opens with an elderly man on his knees.

Much of East Africa was enjoying warm sunshine on a
September Saturday, the rainy season nearly past for
another year. One region in particular was making the most of
the balmy weather, the citizens enjoying their brief respite in the
endless cycle of harvesting and planting. In the hilly southern
portion of our region, many Muslims were getting ready to end

their annual Ramadan fasting, while Orthodox Christians and animists (the traditional tribal religion of Africa) were gearing up for a day of festivities celebrating a local holiday. This odd mixture of religious discipline and secular revelry was creating a small degree of tension among the people, but one man was unconcerned with either. He was kneeling alone in his dark thatched hut, engrossed in prayer.

"Lord Jesus, save my son! He is a successful detective but he is a hard man, I know, and very hostile to you. But you saved me when I was even worse, serving demons as the village witch doctor. You can save him too! Please bring him to the end of himself, even as you did for me."

This man had prayed three times a day for ten years, bowing before God in the morning, at noon, and in the evening. His wife had joined him for most of that time, the couple fasting one day a week to intercede for their beloved son. He was alone now, having recently lost his wife to cancer, but although he was gravely ill as well, he knew that she wanted him to persevere even in her absence. And so he continued, "Lord, bind the demons that torment my son: alcohol and anger. In your name, Lord Jesus, I bind them! Set him free and save his soul."

At the same moment, hundreds of miles away to the north, two women entered a police station in a city that we will call Yappa, the nation's capital. These white-haired grandmothers came each week to sell things. One of them sold socks, gloves, scarves, wool hats, and other items she knit herself, while the other sold gold and silver jewelry she bought at a discount. Neither woman was interested in making money; they went to the police stations around the city in order to pray. They had become well-known to the policemen, who greeted them warmly and offered them chairs to sit on. And while they sat, they prayed, "Lord, save the men and women in this police station. Let your power move here; let your glory be revealed here. Transform these people, both the policemen and the prisoners. Give us godly men to protect us, and change the hearts of those who endanger us."

A man walked past the women, making his way from a rear office toward the street, and as he passed, one of the women stood up and extended her hand.

"Good morning, Detective Dawit," she said, holding his big hand in both of hers. "You look troubled. Can I help?"

The detective looked down at the small woman and smiled grimly. "And how would you help me? Do you have a magic pill to sell?"

"Just socks today—nice, warm ones," she answered without letting go of his hand. Her friend knew what to do, and both women agreed in silent prayer together in this moment of physical contact. "Father, as I am shaking hands with this man, let our contact build in prayer. This man needs you, and he has reached out to me. Help him through me in any way you choose." Dawit, however, politely disengaged his hand and continued on his way.

The streets of Yappa were teeming with activity. Brilliant dresses and scarves complemented the vibrant yellows, oranges, and greens of the abundant produce for sale from markets and street vendors. Even the buildings radiated a rich array of color, as though the city were compensating for the dirty brown that pervaded its landscapes and streets. And those streets themselves were flowing in a torrent of blue, like a river of taxicabs roiling along with horns blaring and drivers yelling.

Detective Dawit walked down the broken sidewalk, jostling others as they competed to avoid the washed-out curb and the long step to the muddy street below. He was a man who did not ordinarily walk with his head down and shoulders stooped. In fact he was both renowned and feared throughout the city for his ruthless pursuit of justice, and the bowed heads would normally be on those who feared his penetrating gaze. But on this day, his heart felt full; his chest seemed heavy, and his mind brooded on a number of burdens.

Dawit's mother had died about a month earlier, leaving his sickly father alone in a distant village and saddling him with a bewildering mixture of guilt, longing, and heartache—none of which had any reasonable basis to his logical detective's mind. His thoughts swirled around the loss of his mother, various financial pressures, his recent disappointment at being passed over for promotion—each scenario colored with a deep sense of loneliness, an unworded knowledge deep in his soul that something important was missing from his life. He felt as though he were standing at the edge of a cliff, his feet unsteady on the slimy soil with a strong wind at his back. It seemed that it wouldn't take much more to push him over that brink.

Glancing up, he noticed a group of pedestrians gathered in the middle of a side street, and heard something that momentarily lifted his spirits: jazz! Dawit loved American jazz music and would often unwind in the evening with cassettes of his favorite artists—the smoky voice of Louis Armstrong, the big band swing of Duke Ellington and Benny Goodman, even the smooth hypnotics of Kenny G or Andreas Vollenweider. His love for the music had even inspired him to learn the guitar, although he hadn't progressed beyond basic chords. But he felt as though a lead cloak had been lifted from his shoulders as he stepped forward in his usual confident stride, pushing through the crowd to get a glimpse of the street musician.

The crowd moved back to reveal a man with blond hair and blue eyes playing a trumpet. This tall white man would have attracted attention simply walking down the streets of Yappa, but his loud rendition of Dizzy Gillespie made him one of the city's star attractions that day. The audience clapped and swayed with the music, many adding their own harmonizing vocals to the mix. Dawit's countenance broke into a beaming smile; although, had he known, he would have resumed his habitual scowl. It wouldn't do for a police detective to be seen dancing in the streets like a common man.

The music rose to a crescendo, assisted as much by the audience as by the back-up instruments on the trumpeter's boom box, and the musician even puffed out his cheeks with the last shrieking notes in proper Gillespie style. His listeners laughed and clapped for more, and he entered into their joyful spirit with a spinning flourish of his trumpet flashing golden in the sunlight. But his encore was not an instrumental.

"Salt peanuts!" he cried, referring to the song he'd just finished. "Everybody loves them. They taste good with anything, and they make you thirsty for more." He was speaking Swedish, but an African teenager translated his words into Amharic, the most widely spoken language in this diverse country. Dawit wondered whether something was getting lost in the translation.

"Did you know that Jesus is like that too?" The white man beamed on his listeners. "He makes everything in life better, and He always leaves you thirsty for more of His presence!" Dawit felt his spirit drooping, the lead cloak settling back onto his shoulders. Another man in the crowd turned and pushed his way past. "Tchah!" he snarled, "just another 'hallelujah,'" using the slang term for Christian street preachers. "Jesus has the answer for whatever problems you're facing," the missionary continued—but Dawit had stopped listening and resumed brooding, walking aimlessly along the city streets; his spirit had returned to the cliff's edge.

And that evening, he slid over the brink. He arrived home to be greeted by his wife with the news that his father had died that afternoon, leaving him with a house and some land in a small village to the south—a place where he had no desire to live. Just a year earlier, life had seemed to be his for the taking, with a fast-rising career in the nation's capital, a good salary, and a healthy mixture of fear and respect from the people around him. Now it all was coming unraveled, and his bright future was fading to black.

He went into his bedroom and pulled a bottle of whiskey from the back of the closet. The first glass numbed his senses but didn't touch the ache in his spirit. After several refills Dawit settled his mind on a desperate resolution. He put on a sweatshirt, pulled the hood over his head, and staggered into the street. His police connections would serve him one last time, he thought bitterly, keeping his head down to avoid any familiar faces. He knew what he needed, and he knew where to get it.

That thought made him laugh aloud, a laugh devoid of any mirth. "If I knew where to get what I need . . . ," he mumbled thickly, "If I even knew *what* I need—I wouldn't be here now." He made his way to one of the city's large outdoor markets, though the booths were all closed and the vendors gone. He knew that there were sales of another type still going on, and he no longer cared if he was recognized. He accosted a man walking toward him carrying an armful of leafy plants. Without a word, he handed the stranger some coins and seized a bouquet of khat, a useless-looking weed whose leaves offer the heady effects of cocaine when chewed. He then found another seller, this time purchasing a small bottle of liquid barbiturate.

He slipped the bottle into the sweatshirt pocket and made his way back home, chewing so many khat leaves that his cheek bulged on one side. "This must be why they called him Dizzy," he slurred aloud, picturing the famous bulged cheeks of trumpeter Dizzy Gillespie. But he didn't laugh.

His wife and children had gone to bed by this time, so he stumbled about as quietly as he could, grabbing the whiskey bottle and a teacup in which to mix his deadly cocktail.

Dawit awoke the next morning, lying in vomit and mud on the side of the street by his house. As his senses returned, a string of curses burst from his mouth. "I can't even do *that* right!" he raged, furious that he was still alive. An irrational anger also coursed through him as he realized that his wife was still asleep and had not missed him. It didn't occur to him that she was accustomed to his nocturnal absences. He tore the sodden sweatshirt off his body, then stormed away in a rage, the stench of his own retching filling his nostrils. With no destination in mind, he strode aggressively through the city streets, strangers moving quickly aside when they glimpsed his face.

"I *don't* know what I need," he thought as he walked, "and I *don't* know where to find it! Hell, I don't even know where I'm walking at this very moment." Suddenly, a song came into his mind from one of his favorite tapes, and words from the refrain struck him as significant: "I will lead you; just take my hand." The singer was blind, as he recalled, and he had always admired the man's rich voice—but now, for the first time, he began to see that the words had a deeper significance, especially considering the singer's handicap. This brought to mind another song with a similar melody line, and one line kept running through his mind: "I have lost my proper place, and now I'm falling out of grace." Again, here was a song whose words he'd never considered before, and suddenly he longed to understand their meaning.

Dawit continued walking, still unseeing, mulling in his mind what might be the meaning of these cryptic lyrics. His command of English was not strong, though he knew enough to understand the basic sense of the words—but their deeper significance eluded him. As he thought about his present situation, he began to see that he needed to discern his "proper place" in life; but what exactly did it mean to be "falling out of grace"? *Grace*, as he understood the word, meant some undeserved favor bestowed on a person who actually deserved punishment. It went beyond mercy, as he meditated on the term, since *mercy* was merely the withholding of some punishment a person had coming. A few of his prisoners came to mind from the past, men whom he had allowed to go free when by right he could have arrested them. But grace went far beyond this; grace would have been giving those men money and helping to get them started on the right path, when in fact they deserved to be imprisoned for their crimes.

Yet how could a person be *in* grace? And what's more, how could a person *in* grace fall *out of* grace? As he reflected on these deep topics, his focus subtly shifted from worrying about falling out of grace toward a concern to find out how to receive it in the first place.

"This is what I need," he began to think to himself. "I don't need a promotion; I don't need advice; I don't even really need family—I really don't deserve any of these things in the first place." This was the first time that such concepts had ever occurred to Dawit; he had always been an aggressive achiever, a man who knew what he wanted and overcame all obstacles to attain it. For the first time in his life, he began to recognize that he had no right to be expecting advancement, success, and attainments; past failures and deliberate wrongdoings began to flood into his mind.

Yet, ironically, these memories and realizations did not depress him; quite the contrary, in fact. For the first time in several days, his spirit felt lightened, and the leaden burden seemed to be lifting from his shoulders. This was not the lightheartedness he had felt when he heard music he loved—that was merely a short-lived emotional surge. This was a deeper sense, a growing understanding that he did not deserve any blessings from life; worse still, he could not ever hope to deserve them. It was a paradox that such a realization would make him feel better, but somehow it did.

More memories began to crowd into Dawit's mind, and words came back to him from other songs and spirituals that he enjoyed listening to. One song persisted, one that was sung by many of the performers on his tapes:

Amazing grace, how sweet the sound
That saved a wretch like me.
I once was lost, but now am found;
Was blind, but now I see.

The second verse to that song had always puzzled him, but now he found himself reflecting on it in a new light.

'Twas grace that taught my heart to fear,
And grace my fears relieved.

27

How precious did that grace appear
The hour I first believed.

"Fear . . . Maybe that's what I've been feeling," Dawit mused. "Fear of failure . . . Fear of being seen for what I really am." More memories came to mind of times when he'd arrested people for doing things he had done as well—the only difference being who got caught in the act and which side of the law he worked for. What if, one day, his soul should be revealed for all the world to see? The stains and stench would be more humiliating than the dried vomit on his shirt, he realized; then some of his despondency began to return. "What good can such a fear do a man? Anyone would become afraid if he faced what was truly in his own soul."

As he was struggling with these and many other such thoughts, Dawit gradually noticed that he was hearing music—live music, not the many spirituals running through his mind. African voices were singing beautiful harmonies to a tune he didn't recognize, but what he did recognize were the words. For this song was in Amharic rather than the English of his favorite recordings. He stopped walking and started to pay attention to what was being sung.

Hear my cry, oh God, and listen to my prayer;
From the ends of the earth will I cry unto you.
When my heart is overwhelmed, lead me to the Rock—
Lead me to the Rock that's higher than I!

The song resonated in Dawit's soul. *Overwhelmed*—that was the exact word. "The ends of the earth" so perfectly expressed his sense of hopelessness and despair that it was as though he had reached the brink of a steep cliff once again; only this time it was the life of his very soul at stake—not merely his physical being. And a rock, a high rock, was a stable foundation looming above the turmoil that surrounded him. He would never have expressed it that way himself, yet it perfectly captured his predicament. This song, sung by unseen strangers, suddenly suggested that there might be an answer to his question, both a place to go and a way to get there. Maybe. He needed to know more.

He took stock of his surroundings for the first time that morning and realized that he had unknowingly walked back to the intersection where the Swedish trumpet player had stood the day before. The singing was coming from a building on the far corner, and two men were standing outside the open door. As he headed toward them, however, one of them looked over his shoulder and saw him coming. That man turned back and said something to his friend, who also looked over his shoulder at the detective. The two exchanged a dark look and went quickly inside the building; then Dawit realized that they had known who he was—and were afraid of him.

A day or two earlier, this would have given him a feeling of power; he would have drawn himself to his full six feet and walked with his eyes flashing. But today things had changed, although he couldn't define how or why. The men's fear filled him with embarrassment. He became conscious, too, of his disheveled appearance and the stale vomit odor still wafting from his clothes; he started to turn away. Then he heard more music.

Bless the Lord, oh my soul, and remember His love:
He forgives all your sin,
And heals your disease,

And rescues your life from the pit.
As far as east from west—
That's how far He removes your sin.

This time, however, it was not the tune or the harmonies that moved Dawit's heart, but the words. The concepts of *rescue* and *grace* came together in his mind, and he began to understand more deeply what he needed. He still did not comprehend how to *get* what he needed—what was entailed in this notion of grace—but he sensed that the answer might be found from those inside the church. In one of the bravest steps of his life (and he was no coward), Dawit moved off the broken sidewalk and crossed the busy street toward the church, unaware of the blaring horns and angry shouts.

It was quite crowded inside the building, the small room jammed with people standing, hands raised, bodies swaying as they worshipped their God. It took a moment for Dawit's eyes to adjust from the bright sunlight outside, and he didn't realize that he'd walked nearly halfway into the crowd of worshippers. But the people that he'd brushed past noticed him; it was hard to miss his tall, authoritative bearing even on ordinary days, and today his appearance and fragrance drew even more eyes. And those eyes immediately widened with recognition. Some of the voices of those in a circle around him stopped singing, and that circle widened as people drew back in fear. But Dawit didn't notice any of these things.

Something inside him had clicked, and in a sudden illumination he understood the words of the song that he'd been struggling with. It was indeed fear that had burst forth in his breast that morning, and fear that had driven him on his aimless walk. He sensed in his spirit that the mysterious force of grace had unleashed that fear; if that was true, then he could depend upon the source of that grace to ultimately relieve those fears—to set him free from the pit. He knew that he was on the threshold of comprehension, and every fiber of his being was tensed with the effort of grasping it. Then he heard a woman's voice: "In the name of Jesus!"

With a thrill down his spine, he looked around him, eyes wide with anticipation. He'd heard the name "Jesus" before, of course, but this time it made him tingle like an electric shock. Suddenly he knew what he wanted: he wanted to know this Jesus, and he was in a room full of people who could introduce him! Surely this was grace in action.

Ironically, what met his eyes was fear. He was literally surrounded by it; in fact the small circle of faces drawing back from him wore that familiar expression he'd almost become accustomed to in his professional life. He noticed a woman to his left crossing herself and muttering, "In the name of Jesus! In the name of Jesus!" A deep sense of shame engulfed him as he realized that she was not worshipping; she was invoking divine protection—against *him*. The singing had also stopped, and he was afraid of causing any more commotion, so he turned to leave. He was not surprised to find a wide, clear path behind him, leading to the door.

If this had been another man, our story might have ended here—and it would have been a tragedy rather than a tale of victory and joy. But God knew His man, and He knew what he needed: a little time to reflect and understand. So Dawit walked outside that church, but he didn't leave; instead, he stood on the sidewalk and listened, for the preacher had started his sermon.

The man was talking about someone named Adam, whom God had created from the dust of the earth. Dawit had heard the story before, along with a wide variety of fairy tales, but this man evidently took it quite literally, speaking of this Adam as though he were a historical figure rather than some metaphorical fable. This ordinarily would have amused the detective greatly, but this morning he was in no mood for flippancy. He listened intently.

"Adam *failed*!" Dawit heard a thump as the preacher struck his podium. "He sinned, and he rejected God, and he *fell from grace*! God had made him perfect—flawless, sinless, without any weakness of any kind. And God walked with him every day, talked with him face to face—God was closer to Adam than I am to you! Adam could reach out and *touch* God! Think of that!" The people in the congregation had been "uh-huh"-ing in agreement, but at this statement there was a loud burst of *amens* and *hallelujahs*.

"Every one of us—everyone here, everyone outside, everyone in the city, in the countryside, in the north and south—everyone on earth is a child of that Adam. And every single one of us is a sinner just like him. We were born from Adam; we live like Adam, and we're all going to die like Adam." There was a pause, and Dawit pictured the preacher wiping sweat from his face while the congregation voiced their encouragement.

"But—praise God! Praise your name, Lord Jesus! We—can—be—" Dawit could barely hear the preacher's loud voice over the rising crescendo of the congregation—"We can be *born again*! We are stuck in our first birth—there's nothing we can do about that. But we don't have to *stay* as sons and daughters of Adam! We can be born again to Jesus Christ, and through Him we can be set free from the curse of sin and death!"

At this, the preacher and congregation joined together in enthusiastic worship, the preacher leading in a lengthy prayer of thanksgiving to God while the congregation voiced its agreement. They joined together in several songs of love and gratitude to Jesus, and for the first time Dawit did not listen to the music—he listened to the worship. He finally understood that these people, these "hallelujahs" whom he had always mocked, had a living relationship with the Creator of the universe—and he knew that he didn't. He was standing outside looking in, standing at the threshold but still outside, and above all else he needed to get in.

With trembling hands, he tore a page from his detective's notebook and scribbled, folded it in half, and crossed the threshold. He took hold of the first arm he encountered—a bit forcefully, as it happened, but some old habits take time—and pushed the note into its hand. A man's face spun around and confronted him. It was the man who had first seen him when he was across the street, and his eyes instantly widened in fear.

"Pass it up front," Dawit growled, increasing the terror of his poor victim, who heard the tone and not the words. The detective tried to calm him with a smile, a ghastly gesture that merely added to his new friend's expectations of arrest and torture. The man tried to pull away, but Dawit gripped more tightly, closing the man's hand around the note.

"Pass this note up front." Others in the crowd were aware of the conflict now, and Dawit could sense panic in the air. Then the Lord took charge. Uncharacteristically, the detective released the man's hand and took a step backward.

"Please." His tone was gentle now, even humble. "I have no bad motives. I'm just hungry for God." The people around him were still uncertain, but no better plan came to mind, so the note began to travel forward—moving from hand to hand. Dawit could follow its progress, as heads and hands swiveled from their worship, and eventually his little scrap of paper arrived at the podium. The preacher had been unaware of the commotion until this point, and was caught off guard when someone pushed the note into his hand. He stopped mid-sentence and unfolded it. Then he looked up.

"Who is this 'Detective Dawit'?" The congregation suddenly became very quiet, the sound of rustling garments and a few scattered whispers replacing the praise of a moment before. The people turned toward the rear of the church, and the crowd parted like the Red Sea. Recognition dawned in the eyes of the pastor as he looked at the broken, disheveled man standing by the door, but he steeled himself, looked down at the note, and read aloud:

"'I'm ready to accept your Jesus.'" He looked again at Dawit, and his face relaxed into a grin. "Well then, come forward, Detective. Our Jesus is ready to accept you too!"

2

MIRACLES

Most assuredly, I say to you, he who believes in Me,
the works that I do he will do also; and greater works
than these he will do, because I go to My Father.
And whatever you ask in My name, that I will do,
that the Father may be glorified in the Son. If you
ask anything in My name, I will do it. (John 14:12–14)

In this present day, God is demonstrating His power as He did in the early days of the church, when Jesus told His disciples, "I give you the authority . . . over all the power of the enemy" (Luke 10:19). He also said, "Preach, saying, 'The kingdom of heaven is at hand.' Heal the sick, cleanse the lepers, raise the dead, cast out demons. Freely you have received, freely give" (Matthew 10:7–8). The miracle of rain during drought is insignificant compared to the miracle of a transformed life! These are ordinary people who are being used of God to accomplish greater works than Jesus did. However, it is not by their power, but by the power of God, asking in Jesus' name that these miracles happen.

The blond-haired, blue-eyed trumpet player in the last chapter was a Swedish missionary named Oskar, and his African translator was his adopted son Jirani. The two were inseparable and loved each other as father and son. Oskar and his wife, Lisa, had adopted Jirani as an infant when his parents were killed in a car accident, and he had immediately become the joy of their lives. By the time he was a teenager, Jirani was able to speak both Amharic and Swedish perfectly, and he had developed a gift for communicating the Word of God with passion and clarity in many other African dialects.

The family lived in a busy town to the north of Yappa where Oskar struggled to spread the gospel of Christ in an area that was populated mostly by Muslims. They had seen only a few converts in nearly twenty years of hard work, and those had come from their annual trips to Yappa to conduct street ministry. Not one person had accepted Christ in their hometown, and the couple had grown very disheartened. They had always hoped to have a thriving church complete with a building to meet in by this time, but instead they had only disappointed dreams. They were, of course, quite unaware of the part they had played in the life of Detective Dawit, nor would they know of the long-range effects of those events. But the Lord had dramatic things in store for them that they would see with their own eyes.

The very Saturday when Dawit had witnessed Oskar's trumpet playing and heard his message of hope, the family had returned home in order to greet a friend who was traveling a long distance to be with them for the coming week. This man was a former Muslim sheikh named Riyad who had become a follower of Christ after reading the Bible on his own. He and Oskar were planning to hold a special evangelistic crusade in hopes that Riyad might gain an audience with the residents more readily than a foreign missionary, since he had been a Muslim leader in the past. But Oskar was thoroughly discouraged, and he was finding it hard to drum up any enthusiasm for what he expected to be yet another dismal failure.

Nevertheless, the three men (including Jirani) arose early on Monday morning and spent several hours together in prayer, asking the Lord to use them in some way to bring people to Christ. They then got to work setting up a tent canopy and a few folding chairs in a field outside the town, offering some relief from the sun. The area had been suffering from a severe drought for the past six months, despite the fact that the rainy season had nearly passed. (The nation where this took place is large, and it is not uncommon for rains to fall abundantly over most of the country while leaving pockets of absolute drought.) People in the region had suffered from the lack of water, both personally and financially. Crops had withered on the vine, and the men had been praying that the Lord might use that hardship to lead people to seek His help. Anything that Oskar did drew attention due to his Scandinavian appearance; as the men finished setting up the canopy and chairs, they discovered that they had a small crowd of onlookers standing on a nearby hillside.

Around noon Oskar began playing some traditional hymns on his trumpet. He was actually a very skillful musician, and his flamboyant style combined with his shocking blond hair rarely failed to draw a crowd, but today's turnout was only mediocre. A number of children came under the canopy to laugh and clap with the music, while some older adults came straggling in out of boredom. The people of that town had grown quite familiar with the missionary's trumpet playing, and they knew that it always preceded a strong message about Jesus; most people thought they had better things to do than listen to that again, and most of the onlookers remained idly on the distant hillside. Today's program, however, was going to be different.

Jirani picked up his bullhorn (they had neither amplifiers nor electricity for microphones in that location) as Oskar invited the onlookers to join them under the canopy. "Come meet our friend Riyad," Jirani called, translating the words Oskar spoke beside him. "He used to be a Muslim, like you—a sheikh, in fact." (A sheikh is a respected teacher of the Qur'an in the Muslim world, and frequently also oversees a mosque.) "He used to lead people in the ways of Islam, but today he follows the teachings of Jesus. Come and find out what he has to say!"

The effect of these words was electrifying, and it caught the three men by surprise. What had been a cheerful atmosphere a moment before suddenly became silent. The children abruptly stopped their frolicking as though they were playing "freeze tag," almost comic in the way they held their positions. The older folks at the rear of the pavilion dropped their jaws and widened their eyes in disbelief—and the small group on the hill moved a bit closer, as though they hadn't heard right. Oskar sensed the mood shift and began speaking hurriedly with Jirani translating through the bullhorn.

"It's true, ladies and gentlemen: the Qur'an teaches about Jesus! Your prophet Mohammed spoke very highly of Him, and he even encouraged his followers to read His book, the Bible. Come closer and hear what Jesus has to say."

A few of the people in the distance began to walk hesitantly toward the canopy, looking over their shoulders from time to time as though unsure how their friends and family might react to their interest. But their curiosity overcame their shyness, and a dozen or so adults gathered outside the tent.

"Did you know that Muslims and Christians agree on many important things? We all believe in one God, the Creator of the universe. We all understand that humans are naturally sinful, and we agree that our sin separates us from God. We all confess that God is perfectly holy and just, and that He cannot tolerate sin in His presence. *But* there is one important difference: Islam offers no solution to this hopeless situation, but Jesus does! The Qur'an helps you understand that you're separated from God, but the Bible tells you how to solve that problem."

Oskar was trying hard to avoid saying anything that sounded like criticism of the Qur'an because he knew that any criticism would offend his audience. He was trying to build a bridge, not dig a chasm. But a speaker cannot control how well his words are translated, and he sensed some restlessness in the audience, so he tried a slight variation on his theme.

"That's why the Qur'an teaches Muslims to read the Bible. In fact, the Qur'an actually *commands* Muslims to read the gospels of Jesus Christ! And that's why our friend has joined us today: to tell you about the great news that's contained in the Gospels."

Word spreads very quickly in Africa whenever something unusual is happening, and the small group on the hill began to swell as people abandoned their field work (which was largely futile anyway without water) and came to see what was going on. For the first time in months, Oskar began to feel encouraged, and he spoke faster and more enthusiastically. He went on to tell his audience that Jesus paid the final penalty for all sins, and He offered that payment to anyone who asked—for free. In fact, there is no way that anyone can ever earn God's forgiveness, he said; it can only be obtained through the sacrifice of

Jesus on the cross, and Jesus gives that as a gift to all who are willing to ask for it.

During the preaching, a few of the men on the distant hill had become indignant and were starting to heckle. Their words were indistinct at first, but as Oskar continued, their comments became more audible. Finally, one man shouted out, "If your Jesus is so great, have Him send us some rain!" He was speaking in a tribal dialect, not Amharic, and Jirani, being a native of that town, was the only one of the preachers to understand the words. He also was the one holding the bullhorn.

"If I pray right now," Jirani responded in Amharic, "it will rain—whether you believe it or not!"

Oskar was not gifted in languages, but he understood enough Amharic to get the gist of Jirani's words, and his eyes grew wide in astonishment. The audience also reacted to his words. Most of the children and adults in the tent clapped in delight, either at the thought of rain or at the prospect of a contest between two gods. The group on the hill, however, burst forth in guffaws of mocking laughter.

So Jirani prayed, this time in the town's native dialect so that everyone in the audience could understand without any doubt. "Lord, we ask that you would send us rain, both to save our crops and to show your glory to these people. Please show them that Jesus is Lord of all creation. Amen." This prayer brought more hoots and heckling from the hillside, and the man who had shouted the challenge stepped forward from the group and began to sing a Muslim song that thanked Allah for the books that he gave mankind: the Torah (the Pentateuch), the Zabur (Psalms), the Injil (gospel of Christ), and the Qur'an.

Others on the hillside joined in, singing loudly, and soon Oskar and his friends had a choir to supplement their preaching—though the singers seemed more interested in their volume than the songs, and there were several different things being chanted simultaneously. (Islam does not have a traditional collection of hymns the way Christianity does. To the Western ear, Muslim songs tend to sound more like chants or recitations.) For a while, Oskar and Jirani valiantly attempted to preach the gospel over the din, but the hillside hecklers added dancing and whooping to their festivities, and soon even the bullhorn wasn't helping.

Now, this African nation has a parliamentary form of government based upon various Western models. The current government even boasts a strong military, but this modern style of government functions effectively because it coexists and cooperates with the ancient African tribal structures. All of which is a complicated way of saying that, in every village and town, tribal chiefs are very important and powerful men (as are witch doctors of both sexes).

This background is helpful in understanding what happened next. The commotion in the field had attracted attention in the town, and by this time hundreds of people were making their way toward the tent and the hillside. Someone alerted the tribal chief of that area, and he immediately feared that a riot was about to erupt. (He'd learned of Riyad's presence in town, and understood that a Muslim sheikh who'd become a follower of Christ could create real tension with the local Muslims.) So the chief hurried out to the field and immediately spotted the trouble brewing on the hillside. He also recognized the instigator in the situation, a local rowdy named Hamas (which, coincidentally, means "zeal" or "fanatic").

"Hamas!" yelled the chief, confronting the man aggressively, "What are you trying to do here? You're stirring up trouble—as usual!"

Hamas turned boldly toward the chief, his face darkened from singing at the top of his lungs. "We are not doing anything wrong," he snarled. "We have a right to sing!"

The chief smoothed his tone with some effort in hopes of calming the situation. "Of course you do. And you have a mosque to pray in." He looked pointedly in the direction of the town. "But your mosque is over *there*. So why are you *here*? There is no mosque here."

"We can worship wherever we want," Hamas responded, turning his attention back to stirring up his friends. "This is Muslim land. We can worship here if we choose."

"Hamas, I will have to arrest you if you don't stop this noise." The chief puffed out his chest with authority, but in the back of his mind he was realizing that he had not brought any of his men to support him; he was alone, facing a group of a hundred or more angry people. He had much authority in the town, and could have forced the situation, but it would take some time to round up his forces—and even then he didn't really want to arrest this many people. All he had left was a bluff.

And Hamas called that bluff. "You want us to go away, Chief?" Hamas said over his shoulder as he resumed his place at the front of the crowd. "Then you make that sheikh go away. He is betraying Islam! Make *him* go away, and *we* will go away."

The chief snarled in anger, but he also recognized that the situation at present was beyond his control. He, therefore, headed quickly back toward town to gather support, intending to return and break up the entire meeting. However, as events unfolded, he did not return that day.

As all this was going on, Riyad got up to speak under the tent, waving away Jirani's offer of the bullhorn. He sensed that his words might further inflame the people on the hill, and he reasoned that anyone who wanted to hear what he had to say was already close by. So he began to speak, keeping his voice conversational and not projecting beyond the canopy.

"I was a Muslim sheikh for many years," he said to those gathered around. "I was very zealous for Islam, and I used to persecute the people who followed Jesus. But one day, I was studying my Qur'an, and I found these verses: God 'bestowed upon [Abraham] Isaac and Jacob; each of them We guided; and Noah did We guide . . . Each one of them was of the righteous.'"[1]

"Well, I don't need to tell you: I found these verses very troubling! Here I was, harming the people who follow the prophets—and all the time, the Qur'an was telling me that Jesus was one of God's righteous prophets! I realized that I needed to know more, but I didn't know where to find it. Then, not long after that, I read this in the Qur'an: 'He hath revealed unto thee the Scripture with truth, confirming that which was revealed before it, even as He revealed the Torah and the Gospel afore-time, for a guidance to mankind.' I suddenly discovered that the Qur'an was instructing me to find truth in the Gospels of Jesus!"[2]

The crowd on the hill could see that the speaker had his audience captivated under the tent, but they could not hear what was being said. They had clamored for the former sheikh to be silenced, but now that he practically was they were more dissatisfied than ever. Hamas thought furiously what to do next.

"Quickly," he said, turning abruptly to those standing near-est him. "Go down there and find out what he's saying." He grabbed the arms of three or four men, one of whom was his brother Jaan, and pushed them forward. "Pretend to be interested in what he's saying. Pretend you want to become a 'hallelujah' too." Jaan in turn grabbed several of his close friends, and a total of ten men moved quickly down the hill to the tent, where they dispersed themselves among the audience.

Meanwhile, Riyad continued to share his insights about the Qur'an. "I had always been taught that the gospel of Jesus was corrupted," he told his audience, "and that no pure copy existed any longer—and this upset me, because how could I hope to read what Jesus said if I couldn't get His book? I finally realized that I had no other option: if I was to obey the Qur'an, I had to read the Injil, and I had no choice but to read the Gospels that the followers of Jesus read.

"And in them, I read about Jesus' death. Now, that by itself did not excite me; everybody dies. As the Qur'an says: 'Every soul must taste of death.'³ But what upset me was the teaching that He *rose again*! According to the Injil, brothers and sisters, Jesus came back to life—*under His own power*! This was something that had never happened before, and I needed to know if it was true—so I went back to the Qur'an to find out. And there I read that God promised to cause Jesus to die, but then to raise Him again from the dead!⁴

"I also read this: [Jesus said,] 'Peace on me the day I was born, and the day I die, and the day I shall be raised alive!' Such was Jesus, son of Mary: this is a statement of the truth concerning which they doubt."⁵

With these passages and many others from the Qur'an, Riyad explained to his listeners how he, as a leader in Islam, had come to recognize that Jesus is truly the Son of God, and that salvation from sin is available only from Him—it cannot be earned, no matter how faithful a person may be to religious rituals. He had much to say on this topic and many passages from the Qur'an to address, and he continued to speak for an hour or more after the ten spies had settled into the audience. It is a sad commentary on human nature to note that, while Muslims were ranting at him from the hilltop for teaching about Jesus, some Orthodox Christians under the tent became angry with him for preaching from the Qur'an rather than the Bible. Yet the Spirit of God works miracles in spite of human nature, and this day was no exception.

For suddenly and without warning, a powerful wind swept across that field lifting the canopy off its legs and whisking it fifty yards away. People scurried about to catch flying scarves and caps, coughing and sneezing, and blinking from the swirling dust. The vacated folding chairs blew over with a series of ringing bangs, while the people on the hill averted their heads and covered their faces. Then, as suddenly as it had come, the wind stopped, leaving behind an eerie quiet. It was then that people began to notice that purple clouds had swept across the sky, darkening the sunlight and cooling the air. There were a few moments of silence in that field, both where the tent had been and on the hillside, as though everyone were holding their breath in anticipation. They didn't have long to wait.

There was no dramatic thunder and lightning, no more powerful gusts of wind—just rain, lots of rain. It came quickly, beginning almost immediately as a strong downpour rather than building up from a sprinkle; rivulets began running down the hillside. In the fields nearby, people stood transfixed, mouths open to catch the water, hands raised in rejoicing to let it run down their arms. Some even imagined that they could see their crops reviving before their eyes, grain raising itself erect, and leaves deepening their green—but no imagination was required to know that the drought had ended.

Back at the meeting ground, both groups of onlookers scrambled for cover. A few of the hillside hecklers headed for home, but most rushed down to the field below. Those who had been underneath the canopy ran and grabbed it up holding it above their heads like a giant communal umbrella, and those from the outskirts soon joined them. But Riyad did not join them; instead, he picked up the discarded bullhorn and faced his huddling audience.

"If there is anybody here who believes what I've said," he cried through the downpour, "let him come out now and join me!"

Without a moment's hesitation, several men ran toward him from underneath the canopy—ten men, to be exact, the very same spies who had descended from the hillside to disrupt the service. Riyad might have become alarmed had he known who these men were, but his ignorance enabled him to grasp each one in a bear hug, roaring with joyous laughter. Oskar and Jirani rushed back to join the sodden group, and they all huddled together as Riyad led the men in prayer. That day, as the Lord rained down blessings and answers to prayer, ten men were born anew into the family of God.

Underneath the handheld canopy, however, the mood was anything but sunny. Many friends and family members of the ten former spies had been on the hillside and now slogged together in the growing mud puddle under the canvas. Some were angry; some were speechless, but they all gaped in amazement at the praying "hallelujahs" in the rain. One of the angry ones spoke up after a few minutes.

"They have betrayed us!" he cried out. "Our own flesh and blood! They have betrayed Islam!"

"They must die," said another voice with a steely menace. "They must all die!"

These statements were received with vociferous anger from others in the crowd, friends and family of the ten young men. "You will not harm them!" they cried out. "They have a right to worship as they choose!"

"No one has the right to speak ill of the Qur'an," shouted the first group, and the debate quickly degenerated into a shouting match. It threatened to become the very riot the chief had feared, but Hamas took the leadership one last time.

"Stop!" he bellowed. "Stop this argument! My own brother is in that group, but that would not prevent me from doing what Allah commanded—*if* he had commanded this! But he has *not!*" Hamas stepped out from underneath the canvas and turned to face the crowd. "Clearly, these people are worshipping the true God," he said. "We don't have to join them, but we must not be against them."

This answer did not satisfy everyone in that crowd, but nobody could deny the truth of the statement. They might not agree with the words of the former sheikh, but they could not deny that God had dramatically answered prayer—the prayer of a man many of them would have called an infidel. A few people continued to mutter, but slowly the crowd dispersed. Most of the people, both Muslim and Orthodox, headed home through the downpour—but Hamas remained behind.

DREAMS AND VISIONS

And it shall come to pass in the last days,
says God, that I will pour out of My Spirit on
all flesh; your sons and your daughters shall
prophesy, your young men shall see visions,
your old men shall dream dreams. (Acts 2:17)

In these days, God is pouring out what He promised.
Many are having dreams and visions of Jesus appear-
ing to them, giving them directions to discover the
truth of His love for them and His redemptive plan,
as laid out in the Bible. Many of those who are having
these dreams and visions are Islamic community leaders. These dreams are often disruptive, causing these
ordinary men to abruptly change the direction of their
lives. And often, too, there is a great price to be paid
in rejection from their community for following the
dreams.

Back in Yappa, the change in Detective Dawit's life had been
sudden and dramatic. For one thing he began reading the
Bible, a book he'd only mocked in the past on the rare occasions that he thought of it at all. Someone at the church had

given him one in Amharic, and he'd begun reading it that very day—starting at page one, like any other book, and reading straight through. He also sold most of his jazz music collection, partly from a desire to cut ties with the past and partly to have enough money to buy scripture music on cassette tapes. And this expense proved to be greater than he'd expected because his wife didn't like scripture music. She'd wait until he had accumulated half a dozen tapes, then throw them in the garbage while he was at work.

And this was the point where the change in his life became most apparent: he didn't retaliate. His wife, Aster, later admitted that she'd gotten rid of his "hallelujah music" in order to "bring back my husband" and to provoke him out of what she thought was a temporary enthusiasm, something that he'd soon lose interest in. She found this change more disturbing even than the black depression that he'd been wallowing in for the previous weeks, and frankly, it frightened her at first. The depression, in fact, had been almost welcome as it somehow had turned his aggression away from her and their children—but this Christianity business was too far in the other direction.

Her husband had come home that fateful day and immediately gotten rid of the alcohol in the house. He quit smoking, and his anger was rarely seen. He would come home from work every evening—and stay home! What was even more puzzling to her was that he didn't merely *stop* doing bad things, but he replaced those old habits with new ones. He began whistling scripture tunes as he repaired things at home that had been ignored for months or years. He became inexplicably patient with their four young children and even spent time kicking a soccer ball with their son—despite the fact that he hated sports. Most disturbing of all, he became gentle and thoughtful of her and was constantly talking about Jesus and the Bible. Every conversation, every little event would remind him of something he'd read in "that big black book," as she called it, and he'd begin telling her about God.

This transformation did not fade away over the next few weeks, and Aster began to realize that something real had happened.

"My opposition began to crumble," she later said, "and my own attitude changed. I began to see things in my own life that were not attractive. It had been easy before to ignore my own failures, because my husband's failures were so much greater—it was comfortable to hide mine behind his. But now I couldn't do that anymore. I finally had to recognize that the effect of this 'gospel' thing was very real."

One Saturday night a month or two later, as husband and wife were drifting off to sleep, Aster said quietly, "I want to go to church with you tomorrow. I want to meet Jesus too."

Dawit's character was changing, but not his circumstances. We cannot be specific about details here, but there were some people who had been pressuring Dawit for a long time to do some things that he felt were wrong. Even before he'd come to know Christ, he had resisted them, but now the pressure was increasing, and his new perspective caused him to reject their demands all the more vehemently.

One afternoon, he headed home from his work at the police station, his head bent low with anxiety, and he didn't notice that the two praying women were seated near the door once again. One of them rose and approached him, extending her hand in greeting, but he brushed past her.

"Not now, Miss Hannah," he said, "this is not a good time."

The women glanced at one another as he passed, then began praying silently but earnestly. "Lord, save this hardened man . . ." They did not know the part they had already played in his life—nor did he—but their Father did.

Dawit walked the streets, lost in thought as he had been that day a few months earlier, but this time his spirit had more hope. He didn't know what the solution was, but he was confident that one existed, and what's more significant, he was confident that God would show it to him. As that realization took hold in his mind, he made the most radical break from his past that he had yet done: he began to pray for God's guidance on a big decision. He asked the Lord to release him from his predicament, to remove the people who were creating the problems; and if not, to show him what his response needed to be. Nothing dramatic happened when he prayed—he did not gain some new insight, no one stepped up to him with a message, his enemies did not suddenly repent of their wickedness—but he did experience something quite new: he felt a sense of peace about the matter. He had turned it over to God, and it was now God's problem to solve; he found that he could live with the problem unresolved and didn't need to be stewing and fretting as he used to do.

The Lord's answer came quickly, though not perhaps in the manner Dawit might have hoped. That very day, a situation arose that forced him to choose: Would he stand firm in his convictions, or capitulate to those who were threatening him? And once again, he sought the Lord's direction through prayer. Immediately, a Scripture passage came into his mind, "But Peter and the other apostles answered and said, 'We ought to obey God rather than men.'"[6]

Dawit knew that his refusal to cooperate with his enemies would also bring radical changes in his life, so he simply went back home and asked Aster to kneel and pray with him. They spent the afternoon and evening fasting and praying, joined by several people from their church who came and went as their schedules allowed. The couple felt that the Lord had concluded one chapter in their lives; and with a mixture of fear and excitement, they went to bed wondering what the next chapter would entail.

The next chapter began first thing in the morning with a knock at their door. People with a grudge against Dawit invented charges against him, and he was summoned to court to answer their charges. The couple quickly phoned their church friends and asked them to convene an emergency prayer meeting.

The court case turned out to be miraculously brief, however. Several witnesses pulled from those people with a grudge and others who did not know the detective at all were called to give testimony against Dawit. But the statements of those witnesses conflicted grossly with one another, and the judge threw the case out of court. Nevertheless, Dawit knew that this would not be the end of the matter, and he realized that his very life might well be in danger from the people who had tried to force him to do something he believed was wrong. So late that night, he and Aster loaded what things they could into (and on top of) a friend's VW bus, and they moved south to his father's homestead.

And three days after settling into their new home, Dawit experienced his first vision.

It came as a dream while he was deep in sleep one night. He saw his home, the little round hut with its thatched roof standing amidst several acacia trees on the otherwise empty plot of land his father had bequeathed. Except that, in this dream, the land was not "otherwise empty"—he suddenly noticed, with the complete acceptance of the bizarre that comes in dreams, that there was an old tent standing in the middle of his yard. This tent was a makeshift device, consisting of two large old sheets stitched together and held aloft by rough-hewn poles, the sides enclosing it made from more sheets—all of them dirty, yellowed, tattered—held in place by more poles made from tree saplings with bark and branch nubs still in place. Dawit's view zoomed into the interior of the tent, and he noticed that there was a puddle of water near the center—dirty, nasty, fetid water that filled the interior with a foul odor. He noticed also that the tent was filled with flies, mosquitoes, and all sorts of biting insects buzzing and droning and whining to and fro in search of someone to sting.

And in that moment, Dawit realized that he was not alone inside the tent. Women had come silently in and were gathering around the foul mud puddle, the insects crawling about their eyes and mouths unheeded as they began to kneel. One by one, the women stooped and drank, cupping their hands to gather the oily bilge and bring it to their faces. The sight filled Dawit with horror and revulsion as they swallowed. His vision then began to slowly zoom back out, rising into the air like a Hollywood movie camera, revealing a line of women extending out the back of the tent, snaking around it, crawling away as far as he could see—a serpentine queue of women waiting to get inside the tent to drink from its septic swill.

The tent faded away, but reappeared in another spot on his property; then that one faded away and another reappeared in a different spot. Every time, the queue of thirsty women followed, and now they were carrying away cups and buckets filled with the diseased water, taking it back to their families. At this point, Dawit heard a voice.

"After this," said the voice, "no one is going to take this water for drinking. I am going to provide a spring of pure water, and I am going to build a new house. And I am going to use you to do that."

Suddenly, he heard the sound of a mighty wind and saw the trees in the distance bowing down before it. That wind swept across his field, throwing down branches and kicking up dust in a powerful whirl. He became very frightened and could feel himself trembling with fear, huddled inside his little shanty house with its grass roof.

"Do not be afraid," commanded the voice in a tone of calm authority. "This wind will not touch you, your family, or your house. It is a cleansing wind, not a wind of judgment."

The old tent was whisked off the ground, shredding its cloth and scattering its poles, and the foul mud puddle disappeared in the debris. In its place appeared another tent, shining a brilliant white as it flapped in the wind. This tent was made from a single sheet of cloth so spotless and white that Dawit could scarcely look upon it. It was supported and given form by many finely hewn poles of acacia wood and, in the way of dreams, Dawit knew without being told that it was not man-made. Inside this tent he saw a spring of water come bubbling out of the grass—pure, clear water, cold, refreshing, and plentiful. The former puddles of muck had been earthly wells dug by men, but this water was pouring forth from the rocks at the earth's foundations.

And now Dawit found himself standing inside the tent holding a big golden pitcher, filled with water from the spring. The long line of women was still coming, but now he was helping them to fill their buckets and pails by kneeling to refill his pitcher and serving the countless women who had come for refreshment.

Then his vision zoomed out once more, taking him high above his property and soaring to the next village. There, beneath him as he descended, stood the same brilliant white tent; he found himself standing before it once again, surrounded by people—men and women of all ages—thirsty for the pure water of the spring bubbling up within the tent. This happened several more times, Dawit being whisked away to a new village to find the same tent; and each time he was met by a thirsty crowd, and each crowd was fully satisfied by the abundant purity offered by the spring. Once more came the voice as the vision faded.

"My sheep are thirsty. Water them."

Dawit was a man who always threw himself wholeheartedly into whatever he undertook, and this commission from God was the highest calling he'd ever received. So the very next day he grabbed his Bible and set off for the nearest town on his motorbike. He stood on a street corner all day, accosting people as they walked past to tell them about Jesus Christ. A few people stopped and debated with him about religion in general, but for the most part people hurried past him with other things on their minds. The next day, soon after he arrived to try again, the town's police officer came and told him to move along and stop bothering people—an ironic role reversal that made him laugh, despite the disappointment.

He decided that standing in the street and randomly stopping people was not effective; he needed to find something more personal and private. So the next week he began going through the town knocking on doors and talking with shop owners, attempting to engage them in conversation about the Bible and God. To his surprise, people responded with real heat and animosity during this time, the most neutral response being a slammed door. There was a high concentration of Muslims living in the town, and a great many were deeply offended at his effrontery of telling them on their own doorsteps that the Qur'an is not the word of God. Many of the residents argued with him, and those arguments sometimes broke down to juvenile name-calling and other ugly behavior. By the end of that week, Dawit recognized that he was doing harm rather than good.

Not long after this, a Christian from North America came to the region and conducted an evangelical crusade. Thousands of people attended, and a great many received Christ. "Aha!" Dawit thought when he learned of it. "This must be how it's done!" He next spent several weeks organizing friends from the church in Yappa, gathering funds and equipment, preparing sermons, and so forth. He and his fellow believers then set up a large tent near a city south of Yappa, and they began their crusade. Dawit and two other men conducted meetings every afternoon and evening, preaching the gospel and calling on their listeners to accept Christ as their Savior.

This time, they managed to offend the Orthodox Christians who lived in that city. "We are already Christians," they said. "Who are you to come to our town and say that we aren't?"

Others felt that outdoor crusades were something done by "those hallelujahs"—it was just not an orthodox method of teaching religion. By the end of the week, the evangelistic meetings had degenerated into open debates and arguments concerning the nature of salvation, the authority of the Bible, and many other questions—questions that deserved to be answered, but nobody was listening.

Meanwhile, Dawit and Aster had been looking for a building to rent where they could start a church. They had been stepping out in faith by doing so, fully expecting that the Lord was about to send them a host of new converts. But they were discovering that nobody wanted to rent them anything, either in their home village or in the nearby town. Word had gone around about Dawit's evangelizing door-to-door and on street corners, and people didn't want to be associated with that.

During these months, Dawit had experienced several more dreams and visions, the Lord showing him many people coming to Christ and being healed, delivered of demons, and even brought back from the dead. After the crusade's dismal failure, however, he had become very discouraged and disheartened. He spent one whole day in tears and fasting, weeping before the Lord and asking what he was doing wrong. "You keep showing me these visions of great things, Lord, but all you send me is failure! I was better off in the police department! Is this what you saved me for: to become a joke, a person of mockery in my country? Why won't you even allow us to rent a building? What do you *want* from me?"

That night, he had another dream. This time, however, there were no dramatic visions, no tents or healings or mighty winds—only a voice. "Why are you crying? Why are you losing heart? Have you forgotten where you were when I saved you?"

Suddenly, his mind was flooded with memories, ugly things from the past—adultery, drunkenness, violence, attempted suicide—all starring him in the leading role.

"Do you not remember who you were?" the voice continued. "Do you not know that I saved you from destruction? The reason that I saved you was to join me in my work. It was for *my* glory, not yours! I saved you to do the ministry that I've already called you to do. So now: stop crying because you can't find a house to rent. I am the one who brought your father home; I am the one who gave you this land. Bring the people here to the place I've already given you! Start the ministry here, where you live, not in towns where you don't. I will do what I have shown you—I always keep my word! But you must learn to do things my way. I will show you how, and I will plant new churches—not one, but many—and I will do so with miracles and wonders, not with the strength of men. And in this, you will know without doubt that I am with you."

And even as Dawit dreamed, the Lord was already working.

That same night, in a distant village to the west, another man was kneeling in prayer. His name was Tamrat, a wealthy businessman who owned several thriving companies that employed scores of people. He was seeking guidance from God on a bold, new venture he was about to undertake with his wife and children.

Tamrat had been a Christ follower for many years. His life had been very stable, with a settled routine of supervising operations in his manufacturing plant, while also coordinating two smaller businesses that supported that plant. But the Lord had come to him in a vision several years earlier (a vision that was strikingly similar to Dawit's dream of the tents), calling him to share the news of Jesus Christ with the world around him. He had been so involved in growing both a business and a family, however, that he had done nothing beyond continuing in the work of his local church. This went on for several years; then the Lord came to him in the night once again.

"You know," said a voice, "you're supposed to be a shepherd of my people. Do you know that?"

"Yes, I know that," Tamrat answered, somewhat defensively. He had convinced himself that he was doing enough in his church and family, while business pressures were filling the remainder of his time.

"Then why are you delaying?" the voice persisted.

Tamrat felt himself squirming with discomfort. After a moment, he blurted out, "Well, I did not wear the right clothes today . . . and I didn't eat my breakfast!" (This is a common saying that does not translate well from the African culture, but you get the idea.)

"Then eat your breakfast," the voice answered patiently. "But when you're finished, put on the *right* clothes and get going." Then Tamrat saw a flock of sheep wandering about aimlessly on a barren plain. "You'd better keep those sheep!"

Yet still Tamrat had continued to delay. How could he leave his business, he asked himself, when things were so busy and growing so fast? And the children—they were even busier, growing even faster—how could he simply pack up and move to some other village without even having a clear plan? Doing such things simply because one heard voices in the night . . . that was just not prudent. Besides, was he not doing the Lord's work right here at home? With justifications such as these, Tamrat continued to dull his conscience toward the prodding of the Lord.

Then one morning, he awoke to discover that he could not move his arms. He spent the day in terror, calling in the doctor to examine him, calling the elders to pray for him, calling the Lord to heal him, but his arms remained immobile at his side, hanging useless like dead weight. At eleven o'clock that night, he fell into an exhausted sleep, and the voice returned.

"Do you know why I saved you?" the voice asked.

"No!" Tamrat's own voice came out angry and petulant. "No, I do not know why!"

"I saved you so that you can serve me. But you are hanging at my side like dead weight. What good are hands if they do not grasp? What good are arms if they do not lift? I have given you a job, but you hang here limp. And I want to give you people—many generations, millions of people! I will give them into your hand, and they will do the same with many more. But now I want you to begin the work, and I will send someone to help you. He will show you how; then you must do it."

Shortly after this vision, Tamrat met an American named Dave Hunt who worked with Cityteam, training disciple makers and church planters. Dave taught Tamrat how to disciple people, to lead them to become Christ followers, and to teach them how to go out and disciple others. He showed him how to coach Christ followers in the process of planting small churches in homes and leading others in Bible study, where people of all backgrounds read God's Word and discover its truth through the teaching of the Holy Spirit.

And this brings us back to the night when Tamrat was kneeling before the Lord, asking His blessing and direction as he finally set out in obedience to God's command to take what he'd learned—and to take it straight to the village where Dawit was dreaming. It did not take long before these two men met, and over the course of the coming year, Dave Hunt and other leaders he had discipled, trained and coached both Tamrat and Dawit in the methods of church planting and discipling that Jesus taught His disciples. During the first three months of their partnership, they planted seventeen home churches in their region. Since that time, this partnership of Tamrat and Dawit has grown to include many other Christ followers, some of whose stories will be told in the following chapters.

4

MOVED WITH COMPASSION

"But when He saw the multitudes, He was moved with compassion for them, because they were weary and scattered, like sheep having no shepherd. Then He said to His disciples, "The harvest truly is plentiful, but the laborers are few. Therefore pray the Lord of the harvest to send out laborers into His harvest." (Matthew 9:36-38)

As Jesus went out among the people we see him moved with compassion for the people. His feelings of empathy moved him. He instructs the disciples to pray to the Lord of the harvest. Asking "send out laborers into the harvest". Later they realize that they are the answer to their own prayer. In the chapter following this Jesus sends the disciples out to serve people—"heal the sick"—with the further exhortation to "freely give". One gains legitimate access into a community through meeting some practical need. In this chapter it is the care for a baby. There is probably nothing as moving as seeing an infant child starving to death. Dave and Lynn are moved to compassion as they "rescue" this innocent child from certain death! In order for the good news of Jesus' love and sacrifice to reach into remote and unreached communities we are going to have to be *moved* with compassion!

While Dave Hunt was engaged in training disciple makers, his wife, Lynn, was working to rescue babies and young children who were at risk of death. In many rural areas of Africa, a young child who gets sick must struggle without adequate health care, and frequently such children never fully regain their strength. Health clinics throughout the area would contact the couple, asking Lynn to visit some distant village where a child was at risk. The Hunts would take the child into their home and nurse him back to health, then return him to his parents.

One day, a clinic called to tell Dave and Lynn about a baby in a distant village, and the couple went together to see what they could do. They found a two-month-old boy named Salam loosely wrapped in a dirty rag, barely clinging to life. The infant's grandfather sat nearby, an elderly man named Mahmud, staring into the distance.

"Why is the child sick?" Dave asked Mahmud.

The grandfather slowly turned his gaze toward the American, whom he had casually greeted when they arrived. The villagers here were folk Muslims, practicing a mixture of Islam and animism, and Mahmud suspected they might not be too favorable to this Muslim community. The people here were not hostile, but they were not friendly by any means. Mahmud stood and slowly began to turn away.

"He does not eat," he said slowly.

"What have you fed him?" Lynn asked.

Mahmud shrugged ignoring the question, seeming not to want to engage in the dialogue. "He chews, but he does not swallow."

Lynn hugged the baby to her breast, so small that he did not fill both hands. "We will nurse him to health," she said, "then bring him back to you."

"Okay." Mahmud did not even turn back as the Hunts left the village.

Salam was certainly on the brink of death. He was dehydrated and malnourished, little more than skin and bones, and unable even to close his eyes. The couple spent the next week feeding him one or two drops of liquid every hour. They gave him nourishment and medicines a doctor prescribed using an eyedropper and gently massaging his throat so that he could swallow. The doctor had warned them that he would be dead within two days, but the Hunts cancelled all their obligations and slept in shifts to attend to the baby, who also slept little because of his open eyes.

After three months, little Salam had miraculously recovered. He had grown visibly in that time, and was eating and drinking like any normal baby his age. Other duties were pressing, however, and the Hunts decided that it was time to return Salam to his family. They bundled him up and headed south. Their reception at the small village was slightly less reserved this time, but not what one would call warm. They found grandfather Mahmud resting against a tree with several other men, leaning on their staffs as they talked quietly. Dave took the baby from his wife's arms and approached the group.

"Look," he said, moving the blanket away from the baby's face, "little Salam is strong once again!" He held the child out toward Mahmud with a joyful smile.

But Mahmud merely gazed up at the American. "He's not healthy enough to live in our village," he said after a moment. Dave was a little startled by this, wondering how the old man could discern such subtleties from a distance.

"He's strong and active," he said, clutching the baby tightly.

"No, it is too rough here in our village," Mahmud repeated, turning to walk away.

"But he will make it now. And we'll come back to check his progress in a few months."

Mahmud looked up at Dave, squinting against the afternoon sun. "But we have no way to care for him. We have no medicine to keep him strong, and very little food to make him grow." He turned to his friends for support. "We simply do not have what the boy needs. You must keep him a while longer."

Dave and Lynn debated this point for a while, but the grandfather would not budge. The group under the tree had grown to include many of the villagers, and most of them were shaking their heads decisively. The Hunts had little choice in the end but to return home with Salam, promising that they would nurture him for another few months to ensure that he was beyond danger.

But when they returned three months later, the scene was repeated. This time the couple were more insistent. "Please," they said, "you must take Salam back now. He is eight months old, and growing rapidly! He is in no danger anymore, and we cannot keep him. Please take him back."

And it was then that the villagers started talking. "We cannot keep him," they all said talking excitedly among themselves. "He is taboo." Everyone was chattering at once, and it took some time, but the Hunts eventually began to comprehend the bigger situation.

Mahmud's son Jamil, just eighteen years old, had been in an illicit relationship with his teenaged cousin, and little Salam was the result. The villagers had been shocked by this and had chased the couple away from the village, the young man and woman fleeing in different directions. The shame of this event in their community had led to a tacit abandonment of baby Salaem. The Hunts began to realize that if they left the baby whom they had by now fallen in love with here in the village it was likely he would die.

"Listen," Mahmud said with finality, "if you leave the baby here, we cannot stop you. But we cannot care for him either. We have little enough for ourselves; we cannot spare more than crumbs for him." He drew himself up, gaining courage from the agreement of the other villagers. "We will just have to wait for him to die. It must be so. He cannot live here."

This was an unexpected dilemma. The Hunts already knew that no adoption agency would be willing to help them find a home for Salam because potential adopters, even from the West, do not want a baby whose parents are cousins. Yet it was abundantly clear that they also could not leave him in this village for he would not survive, so they returned home to pursue other options.

After several weeks of intense prayer, they knew which option they should pursue, and the couple began the process of adopting little Salam themselves. This process took a long time, as it turned out (red tape and paperwork are found in every culture); as they waited, life returned more or less to normal for the Hunts. They did, however, continue to make regular visits back to Salam's native village in hopes that they might be able to establish a relationship with the baby's grandfather and others in the community.

And this was where the Lord surprised them. Their next visit to the village was like the previous ones—until they told Mahmud of their plans to adopt the baby. Suddenly, the grandfather's reserve vanished, replaced with a warm embrace as though they had been long-separated friends. Others soon joined them, laughing and chattering, competing for a chance to hold Salam, taking delight in his every squeal and burp. And this trend continued to grow with each subsequent visit to the village. The baby who had been utterly rejected was suddenly a welcome star, and the short visits grew into long days because the villagers didn't want to see them go.

But more significant than this were the friendships that were solidifying. The Hunts increased the frequency of their visits because Mahmud kept inviting them back, and that in itself was remarkable: to be invited by the very man who had forced an unwanted baby upon them. Mahmud was an important man in the village, and the arrival of his guests always drew a crowd of adults and children to his hut—and the Hunts did not waste these opportunities. Each time they brought with them Desta, one of their church planters, to translate. Desta began to build a strong relationship with Mahmud and whoever else showed up.

Now, there was another young man named Rajiim who had once lived in this village. He had become a Christ follower years earlier, and had been very aggressive in sharing the gospel with his family and friends. In fact, this may have been the reason that Mahmud and the other villagers had been so unwelcoming to the Hunts; it was Americans who caused Rajiim to convert to Christianity some twelve years earlier. After being chased out of the village (evidently a common occurrence in that region), Rajiim had gone to live with some Christians in Yappa, and they had taught him how Jesus commanded His disciples to share the gospel.[7] He had learned much in the intervening years, and the Lord had used him to disciple many and to plant numerous churches.

It wasn't long before Rajiim got wind of what was happening in his hometown because of baby Salam, and he began making a few tentative trips back to see whether he might be accepted—and was stunned to find himself welcomed by his entire family. This time, he shared the gospel in the ways Jesus commanded, first learning to love and serve his family, then leading them into God's Word when they expressed an interest. As they saw the incredible change in Rajiim's life, it was his eighty-year-old father who became the first Christ follower, and over the course of the next two years Rajiim and other church planters planted six new churches in the village and outlying region.

God used the Hunts and baby Salam to begin a transformation in that remote community. In later days, the couple would refer to their little boy as "the Baby of Peace," because he had been the bridge that opened the way for the gospel into that closed Muslim village (Luke 10:5–6). Yet that is not the end of the story, for the Baby of Peace opened other bridges as well. The villagers were deeply touched that this American couple—a couple with children and grandchildren of their own—had cared enough about them to save the life of a child whom they themselves had rejected; that word spread throughout other nearby villages, opening the way for Desta and Rajiim to begin other Bible studies.

With a special burden for Salam's father Jamil (the whereabouts of Salam's mother has never been known), the Hunts went one day to a village some twenty miles away where he was finishing his ninth-grade education. When they arrived at

Jamil's school, they were told that he was presently taking an exam, so they went to wait at a nearby coffee shop.

While they enjoyed coffee along with Desta at a sidewalk table, a crowd of locals came and sat down with them. It is not uncommon in towns like this for strangers to join someone at an outdoor café table; coffee is a very social function in this large nation. But the added attraction of white Americans was so strong that several tables had to be drawn together to accommodate the many newcomers. The owner of the café was delighted with the business the group was attracting; so delighted, in fact, that he came out and joined them himself, providing free refills for the Americans as an incentive to keep them seated there.

It wasn't long, of course, before the large group had learned why the Americans were there, and the reaction was gleeful at the thought of their adopting a son of their community. Without the ability to communicate in the local language, this act of compassion and love spoke to the mixed gathering of Muslims, Orthodox Christians, and animists about the love of God as Desta occasionally injected spiritual statements on behalf of the couple. But one conversation was unique: it was between the shop owner and Desta, and it focused on the concept of adoption itself. The shop owner was astounded at the notion that God would adopt human beings into His family, and even more so that the price of that adoption was the very life blood of His own Son. Before their coffee cups were emptied, the café owner had enthusiastically agreed to continue the dialogue with Desta the following week.

And that is *still* not the end of the story! The shop owner began hosting a Bible study in his café every week, and through it Desta has made several friends who have begun the journey of discovering who God is as they study the Scriptures with

Desta. And what of the Hunts' relationship with Jamil (the baby's father)? As part of the adoption process Jamil had to travel to the capital city where the Hunts lived to appear in court and sign papers. Dave and Lynn made sure he stayed with Desta and his wife during the few days of court proceedings. And as they had hoped and prayed, Jamil became a follower of Christ during that time.

"We had no way of bringing the gospel into that village, nor to so many of these other people," Dave Hunt says today. "The doors were closed, and many of the people were hostile to the Word of God. The Lord used Salam to open those doors and to make peace with the villagers, and because of that the good news of salvation has come to many."

SPIRITUAL WARFARE

Put on the whole armor of God, that you may be
able to stand against the wiles of the devil. For we
do not wrestle against flesh and blood, but against
principalities, against powers, against the rulers of
the darkness of this age, against spiritual hosts of
wickedness in the heavenly places. . . . And take
the helmet of salvation, and the sword of the Spirit,
which is the word of God; praying always with all
prayer and supplication in the Spirit, being watchful
to this end with all perseverance and supplication
for all the saints. (Ephesians 6:11–12, 17–18)

Jesus taught His disciples that they were soldiers
engaged in a large conflict. By teaching that the struggle is with rulers, authorities, powers of darkness, and
forces of evil—"that serpent of old, called the Devil
and Satan, who deceives the whole world" (Revelation
12:9)—Jesus set the stage for His followers to understand events and dreams and struggles in the context of
an unseen spiritual realm where our foe is mighty—but
God has given us weapons for our warfare!

While the Hunts were adopting Salam, Dawit had another vision. He was standing in a desert area, red clay soil stretching in all directions, speckled with green dots of scrub brush. Directly before him stood a red termite hill, one of the countless conical "ant hills" that are strewn throughout the desert regions of Africa, that frequently reach twelve feet or more in height, and that resemble the tower of a child's sand castle. There was no movement in the dream, no breath of wind, no sounds—just an eerie stillness.

Then something moved. That is, something caught Dawit's eye, something inside the black hole at the base of the ant hill. It wasn't exactly a movement; it was more of a shifting darkness, like a shadow thickening or hardening. An electric thrill of terror swept through Dawit as the head of a snake appeared in that hole—a huge head that filled the opening. The head was followed by its hideous writhing body that broke off bits of ant hill as it squeezed itself through, moving languidly yet with a sense of sinister purpose—an arrogant hunter lusting after its cornered prey.

It seemed to take several minutes for this hideous creature to slither its full length out of the ant hill, coiling itself as it came, red tongue forking out and wagging in an obscene manner; but it always held Dawit in its baleful stare. It appeared to be some sort of python, a snake that swallows its victim whole and digests it at its leisure, but this one was the size of a sea serpent with a yawning mouth as big as an oven. There was still no breath of wind, no sound other than the slithery squelch of the creature's motion; however, the air was filling with a terrible stench like the stink of decaying corpses and fetid swamps. Dawit wanted to wretch, to run, but he was frozen in that dreadful dream state where one is paralyzed with fear in the presence of a deadly enemy. All he could do was stare at the serpent; indeed, he had no volition even to move his eyes. It was as though the foul creature had enchanted him, forcing him to watch the slow-motion unfolding of his own demise.

Suddenly, out of the corner of his eye he caught sight of a glimmer, a flash—something bright falling from above and coming his way. There was a singing, silvery *zing* and a rush of cold wind; then a sword stood swaying in front of him, standing hilt upward like a miniature cross in the desert. Its blade was broad and thick with razor edges on each side, its hilt wrapped in leather. It wasn't the sort of weapon crafted for kings in their pomp; this was a weapon of warfare, meant to be used for its potency, not admired for its beauty. Dawit and the serpent paused to stare at it, both caught off guard by its intrusion between them, each feeling the cold wind that was clearing the air. Then the serpent started moving.

In a sudden desperation, Dawit reached out for the sword. He had never used such a weapon before and had no idea how to wield it, but there's nothing like a crisis to teach one a new skill. He gripped the handle of this deadly blade, pulling it from the dirt and feeling its weight in his hands. It was a solid, hefty weapon. He tried moving it, holding it in both hands, attempting to learn how to wield it; however, he had no time because instantly the giant serpent lunged for him, opening its mouth to devour him. In that moment, instinctively—or perhaps through the strength of the Holy Spirit—his hands knew what to do with this weapon of God, and he plunged the point straight into the gaping jaw of his enemy, thrusting the blade down its throat. The serpent twisted and writhed in impotent rage, desperately trying to wrest the sword from his grasp and trying to disimpale itself from the deadly cold steel—but it was to no avail.

As Dawit watched, the serpent began to swell. The picture reminded him of a balloon filling with air. But even as that thought shaped itself in his mind, in his dream the serpent swelled and burst, exploding serpentine debris in all directions. The voice of the Lord spoke in the dream at that moment, saying, "This serpent represents an evil spirit that is placing obstacles in your way, hindering you from planting churches, doing all within its wicked power to prevent you from doing the work to which you have been called.

"It has lured many victims to its lair, slowly devouring the souls of men. The ant hill is its temple: it is very large and looks substantial. But inside it is hollow and dark, filled with a maze of winding tunnels leading nowhere. I am going to lead my people out of that false church, but first you must slay the serpent that is holding them captive. When you do, I will give you a person of peace. I will give you a sheikh, and you will begin your work planting churches among those who are trapped inside the ant hill.

"Only obey my word, and I will do the rest."

In a village about twelve kilometers to the west lived a Muslim sheikh named Luqman. His grandfather had been a sheikh, and his father was the leading Islamic sheikh of his entire region. He himself had studied for many years in preparation for his role of spiritual leadership, studying for eight years at an Islamic mission (called a *dawah*). Then he moved to a city in the south that had a very strong Muslim base to study for another five years. The purpose of the dawah is to train Muslim sheikhs and imams, giving young men the opportunity to learn from an elder sheikh while also learning how to preach from the Qur'an.

It is thus a tool both of training the future leaders of Islam and of proselytizing others to become Muslims.

But Luqman, at age forty-five, had begun to have questions concerning his religion—concerns of lifestyle as well as of deeper theological issues—and his teachers were not able to provide satisfactory answers. He knew the Qur'an inside out by this time, but its pages had long since stopped offering any new insights, and he had become unsure that he could provide any meaningful answers to others as a spiritual leader of his people.

"Doing our daily rituals," he once said in confidence to a friend, "is like treading water: the best we can do is stay afloat. We never get any better, we just struggle to keep from sinking into Allah's wrath." He felt that there must be more to a life of obedience than endless repetitions of the Qur'an, and he hungered to know the Creator of the universe, but he had nowhere to turn for these answers.

One day, his teacher asked him to preach to the crowd gathered under the tents of the dawah. "Only approach the person who has the hat," he advised, referring to the *kufi*, the little elevated skull caps worn by devout Muslim men. "Only focus on those men; they are where you should invest your time and effort."

Luqman stopped short. "Focus on the devout ones?" He turned to his teacher in puzzlement. "But they already know the Qur'an; why should I tell them what they already know?"

"It does them no hurt to hear it again," replied his teacher, becoming slightly indignant. "They are the ones who accept; preach to those who accept."

"But Teacher," Luqman persisted, "if this is a true message that we are giving, then why are we telling it only to Muslims? We must tell it to all Adam's generations—every people, everywhere."

The teacher grew angry with his pupil's impertinence (although the pupil was actually older than his teacher), and he spun around to select another pupil to do the preaching. Luqman felt as though something inside him had collapsed—like the proverbial camel under the weight of the final straw—and he walked dejectedly away. And he kept on walking that day, gathering his wife and children along the way and moving all their belongings in a donkey cart back to the village where he had grown up, where his father still lived and governed.

Two weeks later, on a Saturday night, Luqman had a dream. He saw a very tall man walking toward him, a man who might be called a giant if he walked the streets of waking men, yet without the aura of terror that accompanies the giants of fairy tales. This man had a handsome face, very masculine and strong, glowing with confidence and authority, yet bearing a welcoming smile. His robes were a dazzling white, and his dark beard was thick and long.

"My son," he said, "I want you to listen to me." (Luqman later tried to describe the man's voice, but could only compare it to the sound of rushing waters—"very powerful and loud, yet almost musical at the same time. I wanted to keep hearing it.") "I want to make you closer to me," said the man, "but you have to listen to me."

"All right," Luqman responded, "but before you tell me what to do . . . I mean—can you tell me who you are?"

"I am Isa al Masih [Jesus the Messiah]." Luqman's knees buckled under him, and in his dream he knelt before the strange man.

"In all that you do, you will succeed—if you follow and obey what I tell you."

"Yes, sir," the astonished dreamer replied. "What must I do?"

"I am going to send one of my servants to you. You must wake up early in the morning and go to the old tree on the hill. Wait there, and I will send him to you."

"Okay, I can obey you—but how will I know this person? How will I recognize him?"

"He will come, and you will know him." And in the manner of dreams, Luqman envisioned a tall man walking along with a guitar slung over his shoulder.

He awoke immediately and sat upright. It was still dark, and his wife lay asleep beside him, and he did not wish to waken her. (She suffered from chronic illness—degenerating into occasional seizures and even raging tantrums, as we will see later—and Luqman did not want to risk an ugly scene.) He moved about the hut in stealth, careful not to awaken his family, and hurried out the moment he'd tied his shoes.

The tree mentioned in his dream was very familiar to him; it was a sort of landmark for the people in his area, an ancient *bao-bab* that stood alone on a barren hilltop. It grew a few feet from the road in this arid region, its gnarled branches and immensely wide trunk visible for miles in all directions. To this tree and hill he made his way in the darkness—stumbling frequently and being scratched by brambles—but these things he scarcely noticed because he was so intent upon finding the fulfillment of his strange vision. When he arrived at the hill, he could not precisely see the tree; he could rather sense its presence in the night with that sharpness of faculties that aids a blind man. He sat himself down, leaned his back against its immense girth, and waited.

And he continued to wait. He strained his eyes in the darkness, looking for an invisible servant of this Jesus, but nobody came. He listened intently, hoping for the scrape of a shoe in the dusty road. But he heard only the sounds of early morning—birds waking up, unseen creatures scurrying about in preparation for the coming sunrise. He watched the sky as it slowly changed from black to pearl to luminescent blue. He felt the breeze pick up as the sun rose, inhaled the scents of dust and wood smoke, and shielded his eyes against the brilliance as the sun came over the horizon directly in front of him—but still no servant of Jesus came past.

Other people did come by, however. When the sun rises in Africa, most people have already begun their work for the day, and this was the only road leading from Luqman's village to the nearest town of any size. People walked past him, first singly, overburdened with loads of fruits and vegetables to sell at the market. Then some came by in groups of two or three or more, chattering aimlessly about their plans for the day. Young children went past, urging their livestock before them with whips of willow branches; groups of women went by in their brilliant dresses and scarves—yellows that nearly rivaled the sun's glory, reds that burned, greens and blues that Luqman could almost taste. Less-colorful men walked past, some with surly expressions as they contemplated another day of hard labor in the fields.

Luqman waited through the entire morning, patiently sitting in the same spot and nearly the same posture with a childlike conviction that the promised servant of God would appear at any moment. From the hilltop, he could see more than a mile to his left and right, and he turned his head back and forth to gaze into the distance, trying to discern the appearance of all the foot traffic along the road from the moment anyone appeared on the horizon. Many of the passersby had greeted him as he sat by the roadside, and he had smiled amiably in return, but his attention was never distracted for more than a moment from his intense vigil.

Around noon, his enthusiasm began to flag. First, the dust of the road had dried out his eyes, and the intense glare from the sun was giving him a headache. Second, and with growing urgency, he realized that he was hungry. In his zeal that morning, he had come away without any breakfast—and without any sort of preparations whatsoever. It had not really occurred to him that he might be waiting all morning; his eagerness had led him to unconsciously anticipate an immediate fulfillment of the vision, and the thought never crossed his mind that he might need to plan ahead.

As the sun began to descend, his hunger rose. It increased from a pleasant anticipation to a persistent demand, then increased again to a dull pain, and then it finally increased to take on a personality of its own like a living thing crying out from his belly. "Oh," he groaned, "I am *so* hungry! I must eat or surely I will die!" This, of course, was stretching things a bit, as he had eaten a comfortable dinner just before going to bed the night before, but meals eaten yesterday don't satisfy today, and most of us are prone to dramatics when a strong need remains unmet. "And I cannot go home for my lunch because I must obey the commandment that I saw in my dream, and what if I miss the person God is sending? And I might not survive the trip anyway but perish on the way!"

Just then stars flashed inside his eyes; he heard a *thunk* inside his head and felt a burning pain on top—and into his lap fell a large nut-like object. Like Isaac Newton's fabled apple tree, the baobab had offered him a piece of its fruit in a most undignified manner. He rubbed his head squinting up at the branches above, then eagerly tore into the husk to dig out the so-called monkey bread inside. With a few good leaps, he was also able to reach a low-hanging branch to gather more fruit, and he added a few of the spicy leaves for extra flavor. The meal didn't excite his taste buds, but it quieted his belly and gave him enough clarity to reflect on the fact that there was no breeze that could blow the fruit down from the branches, yet it had fallen into his lap all the same—and this realization renewed his excitement to meet the mysterious messenger of God. So with a little pile of baobab fruit beside him, he settled back against the tree and picked up where he had left off: watching and waiting.

Around three o'clock, a lone man appeared on the horizon, walking slowly toward him from the south. Luqman strained his eyes against the glare, but he could discern nothing—just the silhouette of a man walking. He waited patiently as the walker disappeared near the base of the hill, watching the crest for his reappearance. A few minutes later, he sighed with disappointment and sat back against the tree: no guitar. The walker, however, had taken an interest in Luqman.

"Why are you sitting here?" he asked as he crossed the road. He was a very tall man, thin yet muscular, with long willowy limbs. He had a powerful physique and the build of a man who has labored fiercely under the African sun for many years. And that fierceness communicated itself through his face—the face of a warrior, deeply creased from hard work and perpetual scowls, old scars furrowing each cheek. (Luqman would later describe him as "a very disturbing guy.") He was smiling as he spoke, but that smile was not found in his dark eyes.

"I am waiting for a messenger of God," Luqman answered, continuing to gaze down the road.

"When I came by here early this morning, I saw you here." The stranger spoke the words almost as an accusation, his voice as fierce as his countenance. "Now I'm coming back, and I still see you here. I find this very . . . interesting. Tell me what you are doing!"

"I was told in a dream to come here and wait, and a messenger of God would come. That is what I'm doing here."

"You are a sheikh," the man persisted, glancing at Luqman's beard and clothing. "Since when do sheikhs sit under trees all day, waiting for a message from Allah?"

"Well . . . since today, I guess."

At this response, the stranger burst into derisive guffaws. "Oh, then, this I must see!" And with that he sat down uninvited beside Luqman and began to mimic his head movements, back and forth, left and right, scanning the roadway in search of the man of God. After a few minutes of silence, the stranger could no longer hold his tongue.

"So, seriously now—why are you sitting here?"

"My friend," Luqman answered patiently, "I have already told you: I saw in a dream that a messenger from God would come here and meet me today, and I want to obey that vision."

"This messenger—who is he?"

"I don't know."

Another burst of laughter erupted from the stranger. "You don't know who you're waiting for? But you're waiting anyway—all day?"

"Yes, my friend, I don't know who he is, but I am waiting just the same. And all day if necessary."

"Mr. Sheikh," said the stranger, clapping a heavy hand on Luqman's shoulder, "this is crazy. You should go home to your wife. Maybe she will have some medicine to help you." More derisive laughter.

"Please, my friend," Luqman said, turning to the man on his left, "if you are going, please go. Don't stay here just to keep me company. I'll be alright."

"Oh, I wouldn't miss this! I can't wait to tell my friends about the crazy sheikh sitting under the tree beside the road! This will make a very good story." The stranger indulged in another mocking laugh, then switched to a tone of deep sympathy. "But I'm concerned for you, Mr. Sheikh. You are doing a foolish thing, sitting here all day, when you should be doing the work of Allah!"

"I am doing the work of Allah just by sitting here, I think. He gave me this dream for a reason, and I want to obey—I *want* to wait; I am not angry about waiting. Waiting is good, if you know that you are waiting for God's man to come."

The stranger laughed again, but it seemed a bit forced this time. "But we all have dreams," he said after a moment. "How can you know that this dream was from Allah?"

"It was not from Allah," said the sheikh. "It was from Isa. He appeared to me and told me to come here. The Prophet Mohammed, peace be upon him, wrote that Isa was a prophet of God, and we are to respect his words. So that is how I know this dream is real."

The other man looked at him with a blank expression, not knowing how to respond to this. Luqman, not wanting to continue the conversation, said the first thing that came to mind. "If you are so interested in my dream, then sit and wait with me. But I'm not leaving." He cringed inwardly the moment the words were spoken; about the last thing he wanted was this man's company, and he hoped fervently that he would refuse and just go away.

"Okay," said the unwanted stranger with a nod. "I will sit with you."

And so the two men sat together, silent now, the stranger inexplicably becoming as concerned as Luqman to see the fulfillment of this strange dream. The hours passed in silence, even as the traffic from the morning passed again in its homeward direction, people smiling and nodding as they walked or drove in their carts. Shadows lengthened, colors reddened as the sun sank behind them, but still nobody came past with any musical instruments. The reds softened to muted shades of brown, followed by a twilight grey as the brightest stars appeared above the horizon in front of them.

"I sure hope your Isa is in the business of fulfilling dreams," the stranger remarked.

Luqman couldn't prevent a smile. "Me too."

The light was nearly gone, and both men were getting genuinely hungry—especially Luqman, who hadn't eaten anything but monkey bread in nearly twenty-four hours. A degree of nervous concern, even fear, was also descending on him as darkness approached. One does not sit idly by the roadside during an African night, and this was the time of the new moon when the darkness would reign unhindered. Luqman listened intently to the soft animal sounds around him, scanning the ground nearby for any indication of snakes or other predators. (Had he known the history of his strange companion, how he had once slain a lion, he might have found courage in the darkness—or perhaps have transferred his fears closer to hand.) Suddenly, there was a scuffling sound in the distance that made him jump. Then they heard voices.

Over the hilltop on their left came three men walking and talking together. Luqman could just discern their shapes in the fading light, three silhouettes moving along the road. But something was different about the middle figure; something was sticking up above his head like a pole, as though he were tied to a stake or a small tree. Luqman leaped up and dashed into the road as the men drew closer.

"It's him!" he cried to his companion. "The man in my dream! Hurry—I've found the messenger of God!" He then rushed toward the three men in joy.

But the approaching figures stopped dead in their tracks. A moment before, they had been walking along enjoying conversation, not paying much attention to their surroundings, when suddenly they'd heard a cry ahead of them and saw two dark figures rushing in their direction—and this did not suggest anything good. Before they could take any action, however, they were confronted by Luqman.

"Hello, hello my friend," said this seemingly mad man as he aggressively grabbed and gripped the hand of Dawit—for it was he walking with two men that he was discipling, an old guitar slung casually over his shoulder. "Oh, hello, and I've been waiting for you—waiting all day!" The day's pent-up anticipation burst its dam. "Isa told me to wait for you, and I've been sitting here all day under that tree, and I'm ready to listen to what you have to say. Whatever you have to tell me, I want to listen and obey! Tell me . . . please—tell me now!"

Dawit was somewhat taken aback by the situation, yet he recognized that this strange meeting was not a coincidence. (His two friends had instinctively stepped behind him, but as they realized that Luqman meant no harm they jostled forward to listen.) He gently directed Luqman into a coherent explanation of the dream and his hurried excursion to the tree in the dark hours of that morning.

"And I am very hungry too," Luqman concluded. "Come: let us go to my house and eat together." Another thought illuminated his countenance. "And we can tell my wife where I've been all day!"

"But will your family not be upset if we just show up at your door? And expect to be fed?"

"Isa has prepared everything so far," Luqman answered with the faith of a child. "He is able to prepare the hearts of my family as well—and provide food for us all! And if not, well, it's not my problem anymore. If they are not listening—well, *I* am listening!"

As the group began to move forward, Luqman noticed the stranger standing nearby. Human nature is an obstinate force, rudely intruding itself upon a person even in moments of holiness, and even Luqman's joyful exuberance was not proof against it. He had not invited the stranger's company, he told himself (which technically was not true), and maybe it was time for them to part. It did not occur to him that he did not even know the man's name.

"Oh, my friend," he said with a smile, "please, do not feel obligated to join us. Your family will be waiting for you."

"Oh, it is no trouble," he answered, falling into step with the group. "They have waited for me longer than this before."

"But you have seen that the dream was true," Luqman persisted. "It will make a good story for your friends, as you said before."

"Yes, but the story is not over," he said with a laugh. "And I must hear it to the end. I cannot leave now without hearing the message from Isa, can I?" Then he added as an afterthought, "What is your name, by the way? I am called Koinet."

Long before the group arrived at Luqman's home, they had accumulated an advance guard of children who heralded their approach. His wife, Nahla, was waiting outside their little round hut, arms crossed and eyes flashing even in the darkness. When she saw her husband, she stepped forward with a threatening gesture and began to berate him, but stopped short when she caught sight of the others with him. In sudden confusion, she screamed a string of obscenities, then crumpled into a squatting position, covering her face with her hands and sobbing.

Luqman knelt beside her and put his arm around her shoulders, then looked up at his new friends. "My wife is not well," he explained. "She falls." The truth was that Nahla was demon possessed. Years before, she had cooked up her own religious recipe, mixing liberal amounts of animism together with a dose of Islam and a pinch of Orthodox tradition, what Africans call "Folk Islam." She concocted her own charms and potions as well, many of which required her to also concoct home remedies to neutralize unexpected results. This sort of experimentation inevitably leads to demonic oppression at the very least, and frequently to outright possession.

In Nahla's case the evil spirit generally contented itself with making her chronically sick and weak; her husband had tried everything in his power to bring healing by taking her to clinics, trying every prescription, and even once making the arduous journey to a hospital in a distant city—all to no avail. On this occasion, however, the demon had recognized that the Holy Spirit of God was present in Dawit and his companions, and it reacted with violence.

As the couple squatted together, Dawit and his friends gathered around them and started praying—and Nahla immediately became even more agitated and frightened. "What are they doing?" she whimpered to her husband. "What are their incantations?"

"They are praying to God," Luqman patiently explained. He then told her about his dream and his day's adventures, and he marveled himself as he realized that almighty God had selected them personally and had taken the trouble to send them a messenger.

"And this, wife," he cried suddenly, grabbing Dawit's hand and pulling him close to them, "this is the man of God! This is the man that Isa told me to meet in my dream. And who knows—maybe this is the day that you will be healed! This day, I will obey. And you will obey! And the peace of God will come down upon our house."

Suddenly, the evil spirit within the woman cried out with a hideous shriek. "This woman is mine! Get away from me—she is *mine!*"

Dawit instantly laid his hand on her head. "Come out of this woman, spirit of Satan. I command you to leave!"

"How do you think you will cut me out?" it screamed in an inhuman voice. "You have no power over me. How do you think you can make me leave? I have been here for years, and I will stay here as long as I choose!"

"In the name of Jesus I command you! Not by my authority, but by the name of the Lord Jesus Christ, I command you to leave this woman!"

The evil spirit shrieked as if in pain. "No! No, you must not do this. Give me another place to stay. Send me into another!"

Dawit instinctively drew himself up, as though he were still a police detective speaking to a dangerous criminal. "There is no place for you on this earth," he roared. "You must go to hell!"

With one final shriek that caused many to draw back in alarm, the spirit departed leaving Nahla slumped to the ground in exhaustion. Dawit sat himself down beside her, together with his friends, her husband, their children, and their entire household (which included some in-laws as well). He began to explain to them about Jesus, whom they called Isa.

He told them how God created all things, and how Adam sinned, and how God sent judgment in a great flood—and slowly he worked forward to the crucifixion and resurrection of God's only Son. There were questions along the way, mostly from the children present, but the entire household (which had grown during the storytelling to include several neighbors and at least another dozen children) sat enraptured, jammed cheek-by-jowl inside the stuffy round hut and spilling outside. Many faces peered intently through the open doorway to learn of God's prodigal love and forgiveness and grace toward mankind. They had never heard such stories before, and the concept of grace was more startling to them than it had even been to Dawit himself.

At the end of two or three hours, Koinet leaned forward from the back of the audience where he had been sitting, nearly forgotten. "You must come to my house and tell these things to my family too! We must go tonight!"

Luqman leaped to his feet. "I'm not going to leave you," he cried to Dawit. "Wherever you go, I'll go!"

Dawit rose to his feet, looking awkwardly between Luqman and Koinet. "Well . . . I was on my way to an all-night prayer meeting; I think it would be a—well, a strange thing for you."

Koinet pushed forward and stood toe-to-toe with Dawit, staring fiercely into his face. "You must first come to my house and tell my whole family about Isa. Then we will see about your prayer meeting."

Luqman gripped Dawit's arm. "I am going with you, no matter what! Wife! Grab my blanket! I don't want to leave the man of God right now. Wherever he goes, I'm going."

Dawit did eventually arrive at the prayer meeting in the home of some friends, although the night was nearly past. He had spent several hours at Koinet's home, telling his family about Christ, and both households—that of Luqman and that of Koinet—became followers of Christ that night. Two communities of Isa followers had been birthed, and Dawit had not planned a single detail of it.

As the five men joined the prayer group (both Luqman and Koinet had stayed with Dawit and his two friends), the Holy Spirit spoke to His servant. "You see? I have given you a sheikh—and much more, for in one day you have already planted a church! I will accomplish great things through any man who obeys my voice."

6

AUTHORITY OF SCRIPTURE

Therefore, when He had risen from the dead,
His disciples remembered that He had said this
to them; and they believed the Scripture and
the word which Jesus had said. (John 2:22)

These things I have spoken to you while being
present with you. But the Helper, the Holy Spirit,
whom the Father will send in My name, He will teach
you all things, and bring to your remembrance
all things that I said to you. (John 14:25–26)

Jesus speaks to us through His Word, both the Holy Scriptures of the Old Testament and the faithfully recorded and inspired words of Jesus in the New Testament. He uses His Word to speak deep into the hearts of men and women. God is using the combination of dreams, visions, and Scripture to draw men and women—and boys and girls—unto Himself.

Let's return to Hamas, the heckler who stood on the hill on that rainy day of drought by the Swedish missionary's tent north of Yappa, whom we met in a previous chapter. Hamas was upset that day—angry, livid, outraged that his own brother Jaan had betrayed Islam so quickly and suddenly after the God of the hallelujahs sent the rain sweeping in. To bow one's knees before Isa, this Jesus, was to suggest that there was more than one God of creation. After all, how can Allah be both Father and Son? And that former sheikh who was preaching: he had quoted a passage from the Qur'an about Isa dying and rising again, but he had omitted the very next verse: "It befitteth not the majesty of Allah that He should take unto Himself a son."[8] How can anyone be called the Son of God, when the Qur'an says that Allah *has* no son? Never mind this mysterious personage called "the Holy Spirit" by the hallelujahs. The Qur'an is very clear on this: there is one God, and His name is Allah.

Yet there was also the miracle. The hallelujah had asked his God for rain, and rain had come—within the hour and in spite of six months of hard drought. There was no question in Hamas's mind: such a miracle could come only from the Lord of the universe. Yet there *was* a question in Hamas's mind: Why was the Lord of the universe answering the prayers of an infidel? To get some time and space to wrestle with these questions, the young man decided not to return to his family's home in town that day, but to travel east to a sister's house.

Hamas was from a large family, even by African standards. His father had five wives who had borne him a total of thirty-four sons and twenty-one daughters, although an inordinate number of them had died young from sickness or accident. Most of the family lived in five houses that stood close together in town, but Hamas's oldest sister had rebelled against all that reminded her of the family, including Islam; she had moved to a distant town and joined the Orthodox church. Hamas knew that his father would not approve of his visiting her, but he also did not want to face the scene that would soon unfold when his family learned that Jaan had become a Christian at a "hallelujah" meeting, so he headed east without even returning home.

Hamas's sister Tanzeela welcomed him warmly, but her growing family occupied her time to the extent that she had little left over for Hamas, and he was soon left to look after his own interests. At first he spent his days reading the Qur'an and going through the many rituals required of Muslims, hoping to find some answers to the enigma of his brother suddenly becoming a Christ follower. As time dragged on, however, he found it easy to distract himself in the company of his nieces and nephews, and his zeal for understanding gradually gave way to his daily Muslim rituals interspersed with naps and meals. His sister had a big black Bible standing on a shelf above their stereo system in the main room of the house, and Hamas would occasionally pause to gaze at the gold lettering on its spine, but that was about all the research he did into the matter.

He had been staying with his sister for about a month when God spoke to Hamas in a dream. "Go to the Bible," He said. "Open it. Read it. It is very important for you." The next morning Hamas laughed at himself for being so rattled by his dream, writing it off as the overworking of his subconscious mind still fixated on the revival meeting. The Bible on the shelf, however, did attract a new interest, and he spent a few minutes admiring its rich leather binding and deeply engraved spine. He even wondered momentarily what the book contained, but restrained his hand from touching it.

"It is not my place," he told himself. "I am a guest in my sister's home, and I must not go poking through her belongings." He noticed a layer of dust on the shelf. "Besides," he resolved, "this is obviously one of her prized decorations, even more important than the stereo, so I don't want to disturb it."

A few nights later, he had another dream. A man in brilliant white robes was standing at the foot of his bed. "Get up and follow me," the man said. Hamas saw the man leading him to the main room of the house, where He took the Bible down from the shelf, opened it, and extended it toward him.

"This book is very essential to you," the man said, placing the book into his hands. "This is the food for your life. You must read it."

Hamas awoke with a sense of urgency, leaped out of bed, ran to the other room, and grabbed the book from the shelf. Then, with a catch in his breath, he opened it.

But nothing happened. He slowly came fully awake and realized sheepishly that opening the book was not all the dream was commanding. He began to read the pages he'd opened to: "Just as many were astonished at you, so His visage was marred more than any man, and His form more than the sons of men; so shall He sprinkle many nations. Kings shall shut their mouths at Him; for what had not been told them they shall see, and what they had not heard they shall consider."[9]

These words did not make any sense to Hamas, but he attributed his confusion to sleepiness and continued reading.

Who has believed our report? And to whom has the arm of the LORD been revealed? For He shall grow up before Him as a tender plant, and as a root out of dry ground. He has no form or comeliness; and when we see Him, there is no beauty that we should desire Him. He is despised and rejected by men, a Man of sorrows and acquainted with grief. And we hid, as it were, our faces from Him; He was despised, and we did not esteem Him. Surely He has borne our griefs and carried our sorrows; yet we esteemed Him stricken, smitten by God, and afflicted. But He was wounded for our transgressions, He was bruised for our iniquities; the chastisement for our peace was upon Him, and by His stripes we are healed. All we like sheep have gone astray; we have turned, every one, to his own way; and the LORD has laid on Him the iniquity of us all. He was oppressed and He was afflicted, yet He opened not His mouth; He was led as a lamb to the slaughter, and as a sheep before its shearers is silent, so He opened not His mouth. He was taken from prison and from judgment, and who will declare His generation? For He was cut off from the land of the living; for the transgressions of My people He was stricken. And they made His grave with the wicked—but with the rich at His death, because He had done no violence, nor was any deceit in His mouth. Yet it pleased the LORD to bruise Him; He has put Him to grief. When You make His soul an offering for sin, He shall see His seed, He shall prolong His days, and the pleasure of the LORD shall prosper in His hand. He shall see the labor of His soul, and be satisfied. By His knowledge My righteous Servant shall justify many, for He shall bear their iniquities. Therefore I will divide Him a portion with the great, and He shall divide the spoil with the strong, because He poured out His soul unto death, and He was numbered with the transgressors, and He bore the sin of many, and made intercession for the transgressors.[10]

"This goes from bad to worse," Hamas mumbled, glancing around to ensure that he had not wakened the family. Then he did what any sensible man would have done: he went back to bed. Yet over the course of the next two weeks, he found himself surreptitiously pulling the Bible off its shelf and trying to read its pages. He would first ensure that nobody was watching, then he'd open to a random page and begin reading. And invariably he'd find it impenetrable.

He tried reading from the beginning but got stuck on a prophecy concerning "the seed of the woman" who would crush the serpent's head but suffer a bruised heel—"And who gets bruises on their heels?" he asked the mysterious book. He read from the middle, hoping that the story would have developed in sensible ways, only to find poetry about God telling someone, "You are My Son, today I have begotten You." He opened at random from the back of the book, thinking that maybe the ending would make sense of the rest, but was perplexed by the stories about Jesus, the God of the hallelujahs, dying and then rising again from the dead.

"This is where they get their resurrection story," he thought, "but whoever heard of someone raising *himself* from the dead? And what does that have to do with all the rest of the book? I can't see how these things relate to each other. How can a man understand it?" And, indeed, there was no man nearby who could explain it to him.

Then the Lord returned to him in another night vision. This time, Isa came walking toward him with His hands outstretched, in the gesture of a man inviting an embrace. Hamas reached out to grip them, but the Lord pulled His hands away. This happened several times, each time Hamas trying to grasp the offered hands, each time the Lord retracting them, until finally Hamas collapsed onto his knees in frustration and despair. When that happened, Isa reached down and lifted him back to his feet, lowering His face to look directly into Hamas's eyes.

"Listen to me now," He said, "and *I* will teach you." The Lord then began to explain to Hamas the meanings of the passages he'd read, and much more besides. He told him that He alone is the way to God's presence, that no man could gain God's favor on his own merit, no matter how many times a day he prayed or how much Scripture he could recite. "I am the way, the truth, and the life," Jesus said. "No man can come to God except through me." He explained how He had defeated death when He rose from the tomb, and He opened Hamas's understanding concerning the Old Testament passages he'd read that prophesied of Jesus' salvation work.

"If you believe in me," Isa said in the dream, "I will give you eternal life. But if you don't, you will go to hell."

Early the next morning, Hamas hitched a ride in the back of a lorry and headed back to the home of Oskar, the Swedish missionary. (He had considered joining his sister at church, but she had never invited him during his time there, and he feared intruding.) Oskar and his son Jirani explained the gospel to Hamas once again, and he knelt together with them and asked God to forgive his sins through the sacrifice of Isa al Masih, Jesus the Messiah.

Hamas stayed with Oskar and his wife, Lisa, for a time, studying the Scriptures and growing in understanding along with his brother Jaan and some of the other young men who had become Christ followers on that rainy day in the revival tent. As time passed, the two brothers felt led by God to take the gospel to a town some distance from Yappa that was almost entirely Muslim. The sheikhs and imams in that town were violently hostile to the Christian faith, and the young men understood that they were facing a grave risk, but they were fully committed to obey the God who had gone to such lengths to purchase their redemption.

So the two men moved to the distant town and began seeking out someone who demonstrated an openness to understanding the truth of God, someone interested in studying the Qur'an to learn more about the person called Isa al Masih. This didn't take long; the very day they arrived in that town, they met the man they were looking for. He was a leader in the community, and when they introduced themselves he volunteered the information that he would like to know more about the Qur'an. Since the brothers had made no living arrangements in advance, the man invited them to stay with him for a few weeks until they got themselves established. During that time, he said, they could study and learn together.

Everything seemed to be moving forward with great success—but very few things do in this fallen world. And the young Christians were about to learn the costs of discipleship. It didn't take more than a couple of days for word to get out that two Christians had arrived in town trying to spread their gospel, and the brothers found themselves being shunned by everyone they met. Shopkeepers would ignore them, sidewalk vendors would walk away from their wares, and strangers would glare at them as they passed. Their new friend came under immediate pressure from everyone he knew—and he knew nearly everyone of consequence in that town—as it was considered unseemly for a man of his position to be living with infidels. A year or two before these events, there had been a riot in this town; numerous homes where Christians had lived were burned to the ground. Several Christians had lost their lives, and the rest had quickly moved away. This man knew that the disapproval of his Muslim associates was not to be trifled with, so he told Hamas and Jaan that they had to leave after only a couple days.

The brothers, however, were not to be so easily put off, and they continued to seek out the company of their only friend. (They managed to find shelter in a tiny shack across town—after paying the owner double the appropriate rent.) They would spend hours each evening in prayer for this man's soul, then head to his house on their bicycles early in the morning. On the third or fourth such visit, before the sun had risen, they rounded a corner on their way to their friend's house when a half dozen men leaped from the shadows and knocked them both to the ground. As the mob kicked them and hit them with sticks, they rolled to and fro trying desperately to cover their heads or roll into a ball like an armadillo. After a few minutes that seemed like hours, the mob suddenly stopped their attack, grabbed the bicycles, and disappeared.

Hamas and Jaan limped back to their rented home and stayed indoors for several days, healing from their injuries and seeking the Lord's direction. These were vigorous young men who were unaccustomed to idleness, and their enforced confinement weighed very heavy on them. As they couldn't come up with a better plan, they pooled the last of their resources and bought a new soccer ball to keep them occupied, kicking it back and forth in front of the shack while keeping a wary eye over their shoulders.

One afternoon, as they were kicking the ball, they noticed a small group of boys watching them surreptitiously. The youngsters didn't realize, of course, that the men were more frightened by their presence than they were. But a tentative invitation from Jaan soon broke down those barriers, and a neighborhood game of soccer began and filled the remaining afternoon. The next morning, as Jaan went to use the outhouse, he was met by a half dozen boys, most of them in their early to mid-teens, who had been waiting in the dirt yard for his appearance.

"We want to play football," they said, almost in unison. (Football overseas, of course, refers to what is called soccer in America.) Now, it happened that Jaan loved football; he'd played whenever he got the chance when he was a teen, so the teens' appeal was made to a very receptive man. Without even finishing what he had set out to do, he enthusiastically grabbed the ball and started playing with his new friends.

That evening, the brothers sat with their host in the one-room shanty and discussed the day's events. (Their host was an elderly man of irritable disposition who did his best to pretend that the young men weren't there, and they had developed the bad habit of reciprocating.) Hamas didn't share his brother's zeal for football, but he recognized that the Lord was opening a new door for ministry to their town, and gradually that evening they decided on a new strategy. They would take advantage of the opportunity to serve the boys by teaching them the sports that they were interested in, and wait for God to implant a hunger in their hearts for deeper matters.

"We did not move here to teach football, remember," Hamas cautioned.

"Yes, but we also cannot try to force someone to be interested in the Bible," his brother countered. "Jesus said that we are to be servants, so let us serve. He will open the next door in His time."

So the men told their new friends that they were starting a football club, and that Jaan would be teaching them how to play like a pro. They set the first meeting for the following Saturday, then spent the remainder of the week in prayer. A large group of boys showed up that Saturday, mostly between the ages of twelve and sixteen, but there was a sense of hesitancy in the atmosphere. One of the older boys named Ehan spoke up.

"We like the idea of football," he said boldly, "but my parents say you're Christians. They say you've come here to change our religion. And we aren't interested in that."

"No no," Hamas answered. "We're only going to teach you about sports. We will not force any religion on you."

"I will train you to play like the professionals," Jaan added. "I will help you play football the real way, and then maybe someday you can become a famous athlete like so-and-so [naming a famous African Olympic star]. So we will not talk about religion, unless you want to. If you want to talk about the Qur'an, we can do that; otherwise we just want to play football!"

The faces of the boys beamed at this news, as evidently many parents had expressed similar concerns (although no parents had come out that morning to find out for themselves). But Hamas and Jaan had told the truth. They began that Saturday to teach football and to teach it well under Jaan's skillful discipline, and the topic of Christianity never came up. The newly formed club met several times a week in an open pasture nearby, and many more teens came to play and learn. The brothers, in fact, discovered that there was a real need in that community for healthy activities for teenage boys; far too many were already drifting into trouble due to indolence and the ready availability of khat. Without deliberately planning it, Hamas and Jaan had found a way to meet a deep need in that town, and the Lord used their service to open a door.

One day, a month or so later, as the group was wrapping up their time together for the day, Ehan came to Hamas with a serious expression. "So . . . please tell me: Is it true that you are a Christian?"

Hamas was caught off guard by the unexpected question, but he answered without hesitation. "Yes, Ehan, I am a follower of Isa, the one we call Jesus. Why do you ask?"

"I am very curious about religion, and especially about the Qur'an. I have been studying under many different sheikhs since I was twelve [he was sixteen at this time], but there is much that I still don't understand. For instance, I don't understand why

Christians are called infidels—you guys don't seem like infidels. And I don't understand why you would *become* a Christian in the first place."

"We became Christians out of obedience to God, and even to the Qur'an," Hamas responded, "not because we wanted to be infidels. The Qur'an tells us to learn about Isa, you know. Would you like me to show you?"

Ehan came faithfully to play football, but he was not much of an athlete. He was a bookish boy by disposition, and at the mention of Qur'an study his face lit up. "Yes," he said, sitting immediately down in the grass, "please show me."

Hamas always carried a copy of the Qur'an, as well as the Bible, just in case this happened, so he sat down with his friend and began to show him verses about Jesus and the Bible. Ehan had many questions and made several intelligent observations as they studied, and both lost track of time. Dusk had set in before Hamas realized that it was high time for Ehan to return home, lest his parents begin to worry. He promised to discuss the subject further if the young man wanted to, then rose to leave.

"Wait!" Ehan cried, leaping to his feet. "I want to know more! Please don't go to your house today. Come home with me and teach me more of what you are talking about."

Both Hamas and Jaan went home with Ehan and met his family. Ehan explained to his parents what he and Hamas had been discussing, and to Hamas's surprise the couple became immediately interested.

"You say that your Jesus is in the Qur'an?" Ehan's father asked, grabbing a copy of the book off a nearby shelf. "This I want to see! Please show me too."

At first, Hamas assumed that the father's attitude was like a challenge, daring him to show him something new in the

Qur'an. But as the evening wore away, he discovered a deep hunger for truth in this man and his wife. The brothers spent the entire night with the family, studying passage after passage from the Qur'an, then moving into many passages in the Bible, Ehan enthusiastically following along in his own copy of the Qur'an while his youngest sister dozed on his lap. Sunlight was streaming in the front window of the home and roosters were crowing outside—but Ehan and his father were still eager to hear more.

"You know," Ehan's father said suddenly, putting down his copy of the Qur'an, "I want to follow your Jesus too! Mohammed never rose from the dead—but this Jesus did, and I think that makes Him greater! What must I do to become a Christian like you?"

Hamas and Jaan, red-eyed and exhausted (for they worked hard when teaching sports to the boys), were invigorated with joy as they knelt down with the entire family that morning, hardly believing that it was happening, it was all so sudden and unexpected. That very day they began a house church with Ehan's family, and in the coming weeks his parents invited their brothers and sisters who came bringing their own families. The number of believers burgeoned in their home so suddenly that they could not keep it a secret, and Hamas and Jaan knew it was only a matter of time before opposition would come.

Hamas and Jaan continued leading the football club, and they kept their word to the boys to focus solely on sports and not discuss Christianity unless they initiated it. What they hadn't foreseen, however, was an evangelist from within the ranks—and this is precisely what Ehan proved to be. The other boys had always respected him, both because he was older and because he was well read and articulate. He did not hesitate to take advantage of that position.

"At last, after all my years of studying the Qur'an," he would tell the boys (and Hamas couldn't help smiling at the tone of the wise and learned teacher), "at last, I have come to understand the *whole* truth, rather than just part of it." And he would then explain to anyone who would listen the full story of Isa al Masih, starting with the Qur'an and moving into the Scriptures. And once again, the result was electrifying to the two brothers, as they witnessed a full forty of the boys in the football club eagerly accept Jesus Christ as their Savior. The youngsters were so eager to believe in Christ, in fact, that Hamas wondered secretly just how deep their commitment could be. The test of that commitment came soon after.

Most of the families of these new Christ followers were not pleased with the situation, especially when their sons began attending the new church at Ehan's house. Many of those boys were beaten soundly for their defiance, while a few were even disowned by their parents and cast out to live on the streets. Then several of the adults banded together and went to their sheikh for guidance in the face of this crisis. Sheikh Amin told them, "Do not panic. I will attend to this."

This sheikh had not been idle over the previous few months since the brothers arrived in his town. He had been in contact with his superiors at a large mosque in Yappa, and had already started making plans for how to get rid of them—peacefully if possible, but by force if needed. He had been involved personally in the riots, arson, and murders against Christians that had happened a few years earlier—and such deeds come easier the second time. He was, in the words of Hamas, "a very, very dangerous guy." But when it came to the members of his own mosque, more subtlety was called for.

Sheikh Amin began to hover about nearby whenever the football club got together, waiting for an opportunity to catch one or two of the boys by themselves. He would walk with them on their way to practice, walk them home in the afternoon, pull them aside when they were not playing, grabbing every chance to whisper in their ears and insinuate into their hearts that Christianity is an abomination in the eyes of Islam.

"Don't you know that Christians are cannibals?" he would say in an incredulous tone. "They eat human flesh and drink human blood!" (This idea was evidently drawn from his limited understanding of the Lord's communion service.) "These Christians," he would say to the younger boys, "they just want to get you away from your families so they can sell you into slavery! You'll see! If you don't come back to mosque, you will soon find yourself riding camels in Arabia!"

Amin had some success intimidating a few, but most of the boys laughed and a few of the older ones mocked him openly. They knew Hamas and Jaan too well to believe such absurd claims and, sad to say, a few of them were enjoying the rebellious sense of independence in attending a church against their parents' wishes. So Amin needed to find a more effective method, and it didn't require much imagination to do so. A quick phone call to Yappa was all he needed; then he put his plan into action.

At the next gathering of the football club, Amin waited until all the boys were gathered; then he strode into the midst of them with a bold defiance. Hamas and Jaan, not wanting to incite any trouble, quietly stepped back a few paces—although it made Hamas seethe inwardly to back down from a confrontation. (One's human nature, after all, may become subjugated, but it never fully goes away.) This gesture was not lost on Amin, and the thought that he had dominated the Christians lent a lurid glow to his countenance as he beamed triumphantly at the boys around him.

"Boys," he proclaimed in a stentorian voice, "I have wonderful news for you! If you will come back to Islam and return to your mosque, I will give you . . ." he paused dramatically . . . "ten thousand birr each!" This would be roughly equivalent to six hundred dollars US, an unimaginable fortune to most of those boys—and they stood around him in stunned silence. But Amin was not finished, and he continued his sales pitch like P. T. Barnum. "And not only that—*not only that!*—but I will take you to Yappa, and from there you will fly—*on an airplane!*—you will fly to . . . *Mecca!*" There was a collective gasp as the boys tried to imagine themselves flying—on an airplane, no less—to the Islamic holy city. A few of the older boys already had plans on how to spend their pending fortune, many in ways that might be frowned upon in Mecca. But Amin still had one more arrow in his quiver, and he had saved what he thought the best for last.

"And while you are in Mecca," he said, lowering his voice dramatically, leaning his face close to the boys, and turning slowly in a circle to face each one—looking for all the world like Fagin from *Oliver Twist*—"while you are in Mecca, you will be trained to become *sheikhs!*" This last item proved anticlimactic for most of the boys, but nothing could dim their visions of grandeur, and there was much bustling and excited chatter in the crowd. Hamas stood near the fringe of the group, outrage welling up within him. He wanted to strike out, to charge through the crowd like a bull and gore his adversary; but words kept nagging his mind: "He opened not His mouth . . . He opened not His mouth." He could only glare in angry disbelief at several boys who had recently seemed so enthusiastic about growing in their newfound faith, while Jaan stood beside him silently praying.

Over the next few days, more and more of the new Christians in the club quietly went with their parents to the mosque to accept the sheikh's offer, and by the end of the week most of them had done so. Amin had chartered a bus with the help of the imams at the mosque in Yappa (a very rare extravagance, but deemed worthwhile by the leaders of the parent mosque for their own reasons), and the following Saturday it rattled out of town carrying about thirty-five of the new Christians, overseen by Sheikh Amin.

Hamas and Jaan were heartbroken, but they did not give up the battle. They called together the believers who met with them at Ehan's home (Ehan had scorned the sheikh's offer) and held an all-night prayer meeting that very evening and three times a week thereafter, each family fasting at least one day a week as they were able. They made a list of the boys who had been seduced onto the bus and prayed for each by name, asking God to protect them and show them the truth. They also prayed for the family of each boy and for the town in general, that the Lord's truth would become powerfully clear. And they did not fail to pray for Sheikh Amin, regardless of what emotions were stirred in the process.

And twenty days later, without any fanfare or advance notice, the bus came rattling back into town, carrying all thirty-five boys—with Sheikh Amin sitting dejectedly in the front. Over the next few days, Hamas was able to piece together what had happened.

Prior to the trip, Sheikh Amin had been in contact with the primary leader of one of the largest mosques in Yappa, a man named Sheikh Jambres. He initially had received little in the way of encouragement or advice, even though he had been personally trained by Sheikh Jambres years before. But then Jambres had called him back to propose the scheme of paying the boys and sending them en masse to Mecca for training, telling him that there was a group of Arab missionaries working with him at the mosque who would underwrite the plan. This was an unlooked-for blessing that sounded too good to be true, but Amin in desperation had ultimately accepted.

The boys had been placed under the authority of a wealthy young couple who owned a large villa in Yappa. They had been housed in a back room with no windows where they spent virtually the entire twenty days—well fed and cared for, but only venturing outside the home to use the latrine. At first, the mosque would send a sheikh to the home to educate the boys on the Qur'an (although he spent most of his time railing against Christianity and the infidels who follow it), but within a week even these visits petered out.

Amin, meanwhile, had arrived expecting cash and plane tickets for each boy; when neither materialized, he had spent most of two weeks trying to meet with Sheikh Jambres or at least one of his assistants. These men proved very elusive, and on the rare occasions when Amin managed to corner one of them, he would turn out to be strangely ignorant of the entire affair. Once or twice, he buttonholed Sheikh Jambres and pressed him to send the boys to Mecca, but the sheikh only promised to meet with him the next afternoon to discuss it—meetings that never occurred.

By the third week, Amin had begun pursuing the Arab missionaries since they were the ones allegedly paying for the whole trip, but he found them to be icy and aloof, and they seemed to have a profound difficulty with the language barrier.

He became so frustrated that he resorted to simply begging any-one and everyone he met around the mosque to help him send the boys off.

"These boys—almost forty of them!—they were brought up to be good Muslims, but they got led away by Christians and abandoned Allah. But now they have returned to Islam, and we need to help them. Won't you help them?" But the results were always the same.

One day, Amin returned to the house to find an imam shaking one of the boys, slapping him and screaming. Amin interposed, and the imam left in his rage.

"What is the meaning of this, Sisay?" he asked the boy.

"I asked the imam a question," he answered between sobs.

"Well," Amin said, trying clumsily to help the boy laugh, "it must have been a tough one, eh? To make the imam so angry? What did you ask?"

"I showed him a verse in the Qur'an and asked him to explain it, that's all!"

Amin scowled and paused, suspecting that there was a good deal more to the story. "You are saying, then, that the imam got angry because you asked him to explain the Qur'an? Come now . . . tell me true."

"I *am* telling you true," the boy insisted indignantly, grab-bing a nearby Qur'an. "I showed him this verse: 'The Messiah, Jesus Son of Mary, was only a messenger of Allah, and His word which He conveyed unto Mary, and a spirit from Him.'[11]

"Then I asked him, 'Why do you teach us that Isa is just a man, when the Qur'an says that he is the word of God, and a spirit that comes from God?' And he yelled, 'Look at the rest of it, boy! Look at the rest of it!' And so I read on, which says: 'So believe in Allah and His messengers, and say not

"Three"—Cease! It is better for you! Allah is only One Allah. Far is it removed from His Transcendent Majesty that He should have a son.'"

The young boy paused to rub some tears from his eyes, Amin suspecting that he was making the most of the unexpected attention. "So what happened then?" he asked after a moment.

"Well," the boy said between forced sobs, "I said, 'But if Isa is Allah's messenger, aren't we supposed to listen to what he says?'"

"Yes . . . and then?"

"And then he started shouting."

Amin, with a tangle of emotions, had to disguise a smile at the dramatized explanation. But then his face grew grave. "Why do you raise such verses from the Qur'an? And how did you find this verse?"

"Ehan showed it to me."

Amin sighed and rolled his eyes. "Listen, you forget the things that Ehan said. He does not know. He is not a sheikh; he is not an imam—but someday you *will* be, and then you can go and tell *him* something."

Sisay stared intently into Amin's eyes for a moment with a fixed expression. "We are not going to be sheikhs, and you know it."

Amin was fully taken aback this time. Little Sisay was turning out to be disturbingly perceptive. But he could not let the boys know how discouraged he, too, was becoming with the entire situation, so he resorted to old habit: he bluffed. "Of course you are, Sisay," he said, a bit more loudly than necessary. (The entire group of boys was still huddled in one corner, not yet recovered from the fear of Sisay's beating.) "I am working every day on getting you to Mecca—it's just taking a little longer than I expected, that's all."

Sisay nearly spat with disgust at this. "Pfah! Sent to Mecca! Do they buy slaves in Mecca?"

Amin, for perhaps the first time in his life, was struck dumb. "What?"

"That is what they're doing, Sheikh Amin! That is why we're hidden in this room. That is why the Arab missionaries are here. That is why you brought us here!"

Amin was stunned. It was an outrageous suggestion—criminal even, had it been made by an adult, and certainly worthy of some stern discipline—yet something in his spirit told him it was true. But until he had the facts, the present situation called for immediate bluster. "Sisay, you are making trouble! Never read this part of the Qur'an, and do not ask such questions among these people! Understood?"

Child slavery is very real and very prevalent in many places around the world, even in our allegedly "enlightened" times. Children between the ages of ten and eighteen are prime targets of slave traders, although they will take children of any age if they can manage it. Infants are stolen and sold to illicit adoption agencies, while young boys are sold as jockeys for camel races. Girls of any age, of course, are forced into prostitution—and these rings sell their victims all over the world, including into the United States and Europe. In this part of Africa, boys like Sisay and his friends are most commonly sold to Arab countries to become domestic servants or camel jockeys, although many are also sold right within Africa to work as unpaid laborers in weaving mills. And how much are these human beings sold for—these who are made in the image of their Creator, with eternal souls and the capacity for love and godliness? The going price is around fifty dollars!

Sheikh Amin knew all these things, and a great deal more—for historically Muslims account for much of the traffic, both buying and selling—and he was deeply disturbed. In spite of his violent zeal for his religion, Amin was not a wicked man. Dangerous, yes, but his crimes were committed under the self-delusion that he was serving almighty God, and his conscience was still active. If these charges were true, he reflected, then he was fully complicit in the destruction of thirty-five innocent lives; worse still, their parents had entrusted them into his care in the full expectation that he had their best interests in hand. His bile rose at the thought of betraying that trust, and with it came a great anger—ironically directed against the very man whom he admired more than any other: Sheikh Jambres, who had made him the man he was.

So Amin made some discreet inquiries that very evening, phoning some trustworthy friends in Yappa and asking careful questions of people in the mosque. In a few hours, he was fully convinced that little Sisay was one very perceptive boy. Without losing a minute, he went into the street and hired half a dozen of the blue VW vans that serve as cabs in Yappa—emptying his pockets in the process—and led them to the house where the boys were being kept. He loaded them into the cabs, took them to the bus depot, and spent the rest of the night calling in favors and debts from every quarter, the boys sleeping on the floor as best they could. By 6 a.m., he had gathered enough to barter a hired bus back to his town, where he led his charges home like a broken shepherd.

About a week after the boys returned, Hamas learned that the leaders of the Yappa mosque had issued a *fatwa* that called for a death sentence against him and Jaan. He knew that this was a very real threat, and he did not take it lightly—but he did not panic either. Instead, he gathered his fellow believers together once again, and they refocused their thrice-weekly all-night prayer meetings to meet the crisis. They also gathered daily, as many as could come, to pray and fast with tears. They prayed, "Lord, reveal your glory among this community, among this nation, and let them know you. We pray for Sheikh Amin, and thank you for moving him to return the boys safely. Do not give up on him, Lord—lead him to yourself. We also pray that you will expose the truth to Sheikh Jambres and his assistants, to the Arab missionaries who trade in human flesh, to the many whose names we don't even know who help these people in their wickedness—we pray that you would bring them to their knees in repentance. Lord, we pray that you will close this mosque in Yappa; shut it down, Lord, and leave it shut down!"

They continued this daily prayer vigil for ten days, sometimes praying through the entire night, and they had no intention of stopping. Then a rumor reached them that the mosque in Yappa had been suddenly closed. And with a few phone calls, Ehan's father confirmed that it was true. They did not know the reason, but they rejoiced in the grace of God that answers prayer. Only later did they find out what had happened.

Several days after issuing the *fatwa*, Sheikh Jambres entered the mosque to prepare for morning prayers. He was bending down smoothing out his prayer mat (for he was a fastidious man) when a searing pain shot up his leg. He spun around to the horrific vision of a huge mamba, one of the deadliest snakes in Africa, removing its fangs from his right calf. It was easily eight feet long, of a pale olive color, twisting and sliding along the floor, a hideous and disgusting and repulsive creature of nightmares—and it was coming at him for another taste!

He leaped up screaming and thrashed about, flailing his arms over his head, shrieking incoherently, trying to lift both bare feet off the floor simultaneously, and effectively speeding the course of the deadly venom into his blood stream. And still the viper came for him.

Now, the black mamba is the fastest snake in the world, clocked at speeds over ten miles per hour; it is very aggressive toward anything that enters whatever territory it has claimed for itself—and this serpent had evidently claimed Jambres's worship space—but the snake was no match for the speed Sheikh Jambres made that morning. He hiked up his skirts, threw back his head in a banshee howl, and went whistling out of the building, knocking over an elderly man on his way.

People had begun arriving at the mosque for prayer. But they leaped back in alarm at the sight of their high priest roaring out the front door as though the devil himself were in pursuit, robes pulled up above his knees, hair blowing straight out behind. Your average African does not need to ask questions to know when someone is fleeing a snake, and these early arrivers followed the example of their sheikh—for the last time, as it turned out—and took to their heels. Word spread very quickly that there was a mamba slithering through the darkness inside their mosque, and the building remained completely empty of human souls, deserted even by its imams and sheikhs and most faithful adherents.

Fortunately for Sheikh Jambres, most clinics in this part of Africa are equipped with an anti-venom serum that neutralizes the poison of the mamba, and in Yappa there are many such clinics. He was able to get help in time to save his life, although the next few days proved very unpleasant and painful in debilitating ways—the details of which we will spare you. Evidently, as he was writhing in the hospital, he had time to reflect on his priorities and on his future; a drastic change seemed in order. The day that Jambres was released, he went to the home of another man, took his wife for himself, and ran off with her to some other area to set up housekeeping. This proved to be the final demise for his mosque. In time, the people would have rid themselves of the snake, but they could not easily rid themselves of this deep betrayal by their sheikh.

"We will not go to this mosque anymore," was the common lament, "because the sheikhs are stealing our wives." And it remains closed to this day.

And what became of the thirty-five boys who were seduced to Yappa? Every one of them, singly or in pairs, came to Hamas and Jaan and asked them to pray that Jesus would forgive their unfaithfulness.

7

SCRIPTURE STORIES

*In the beginning God created the
heavens and the earth. (Genesis 1:1)*

Scripture stories that begin with creation are often the best way to engage a new people group. One begins by sharing each culture's creation stories, and the stories then move through the Bible to the stories of Jesus Christ. This method is called "Creation to Christ Bible Story Telling." In some places in Africa, as towns and villages are transformed through disciple making and the emergence of simple spiritual communities, other community leaders will see the transformation and ask for "the storytellers" to come to their communities.

Koinet, the man who joined Luqman under a tree in chapter 5, was a member of the Maasai people. The Maasai are fierce nomads of the mountain regions, famous for their jumping dance in which young men leap straight into the air, as well as their deadly long spears and colorful oval shields. They believe that God ordained for all cattle on earth to be the natural inheritance of the Maasai people, and any person who owns a cow holds it illegitimately; the cow is the birthright of any

Maasai tribesman who chooses to "liberate" it from its captivity and take it for his own.

Koinet had inherited his people's stern and assertive outlook on life as well as their tall physique, and this had earned him the nickname Koinet in later life (for it was not his real name), meaning "tall one." But his height was not what made him seem so fierce to people he met; the fact is, he really *was* fierce and had developed a reputation even as a boy for a short temper and quick fists. When he came of age, he had proven his manhood in the traditional Maasai manner by killing a lion. Yet his penchant for trouble and conflict did not endear him to his tribe; after a particularly violent outburst, he had been forced to leave. He had wandered far afield before marrying and settling down.

Not long after becoming a follower of Christ, Koinet felt that he needed to make things right with the people he had left behind in his homeland, so he and his wife gathered their children and belongings and headed south. They took up residence in the new region, and Koinet made contact with a friend of Dawit's named Ita. There were several tribes of Maasai in the mountains surrounding the region, groups that were not nomadic like other Maasai, and Ita had wanted to teach them about Christ—but he did not know how to gain access to their villages. Koinet, on the other hand, wanted to find his family's nomadic tribe, which also was likely in the mountains, and the men felt that they might accomplish both tasks by working together. So, after a time of prayer and preparation, the two men set out on a trek joined by two of Ita's co-workers.

They spent the first two or three days hiking through increasingly mountainous terrain, sometimes walking on a well-worn path, more frequently clambering through sharp outcroppings of rock and loose scree. There were few trees, for the land was sharp and jagged, and what greenery existed was mostly scrub. But on the fourth day, as they trudged out of a valley under the noontime sun, they spotted a lone acacia tree. With a burst of excitement, the four men dropped down in its shade, chatting happily as they shared some cool papaya for lunch.

After a few minutes, Koinet noticed that they had an audience: a young man, about twenty yards away, stood silently on his right foot, the left leg crooked with foot resting against the right knee, leaning on a very long spear with a stick resting on a shoulder, intently watching them. He was barely clothed with only a thin blanket wrapped around his mid-section, his skin gleaming black in the sun. The men quickly recognized him as a Maasai goatherd, and they turned back to their conversation and paid him no more attention. (It seems odd now that they did not recognize an opportunity when it was offered, but the human needs of fatigue and hunger had somehow seemed more important at the moment.) Their snub was not returned, however, as the young man's curiosity at seeing three strangers in such a remote spot overcame his natural shyness; he gradually moved closer and closer, until he was standing just outside the tree's shade.

"Who are you?" he asked abruptly. The men were startled to find him standing so close by, and even somewhat alarmed, but Koinet recovered his self-possession and introduced himself and his friends. He explained, upon further questioning from their guest, that they were on their way to tell the Maasai people the good news about Jesus Christ and His free gift of salvation.

"Free gift?" the young man asked (whose name was Lembui), his face brightening with interest. Ita assumed that the promise of anything free was what motivated Lembui's curiosity, as well as the novelty of chatting with traveling strangers and hearing new stories—but Koinet was finally awakening to the unexpected opportunity.

"God offers a free gift of salvation," Koinet explained, casually offering some papaya to their guest.

"What is salvation?" Lembui promptly asked.

"It means . . . it means forgiveness from sin . . . and eternal life in heaven."

"What is sin?" Lembui asked, sitting himself down with the group without an invitation.

"Sin is . . ." Koinet glanced at his friends. "Well, sin is doing what is wrong in God's eyes. Stealing things, hurting people . . . stuff like that."

"What makes those things wrong? What makes something 'mine' or 'yours' in the first place? And what if two people disagree? Who decides which one is right?"

"Well," Koinet answered after a pause to scratch his head, "God's Word tells us what is right and what is wrong. And I guess—"

"What is God's Word?"

The best way to master a subject is to try teaching it, and Koinet was discovering that he had much to learn, for Lembui's questions were not those of mere idle curiosity. After a few minutes, he said, "Look, let's start at the beginning. Who created the earth and all the living creatures?"

"Well," Lembui answered slowly, "in the beginning, Enkai made all things—both Black Enkai and Red Enkai." (The Maasai believe that there is one god with a dual nature, one good and one evil, similar to Eastern notions of *yin* and *yang*.) "Red Enkai and Black Enkai fought together; they struggled with each other for a very, very long time, and that chaos brought forth all there is."

"In my story of creation," Koinet said after a brief pause, "there is one God, and He existed alone before anything was made. He alone created all things, but He did it simply by speaking. He said, 'Let there be light,' and light appeared. He did not struggle to do it, there was no chaos or fighting—there was nobody else involved at all—just Him." The conversation continued along these lines for a good while as the men ate fruit in the shade of the tree.

After a time, Lembui said, "Our stories are similar, yet I think that somehow the differences are very important." Koinet handed him an orange, which he began to peel abstractedly, his mind wrestling with questions. "I do not have the wisdom of my elders—I'm only eighteen—and I have no education. But still . . . it seems to me that whoever created me is my god, because he is the one that I must answer to for the life that he gave me."

So Koinet began with Genesis 1, explaining to Lembui how God created the entire universe in six days, and moving on to explain the origin of all sin on the day when Adam ate the fruit that God had forbidden. The group sat together under that tree for the entire afternoon; Koinet and his friends told stories from the Bible while Lembui asked probing questions, and slowly the gospel was unfolded to the young mountain goatherd.

"I believe what you are saying is true," Lembui stated as the sun was sinking behind the mountaintops. "Please, come to my house for the night before it gets dark. I want you to tell my mother about these things—we will both want to know more about your Jesus."

And so it happened that Koinet and his friends found their way to one of the Maasai tribes through an unexpected channel, joining Lembui and his mother in their round mud hut. They sat up most of the night retelling the same stories, and telling other stories from the Gospels, and before daybreak both Lembui and his mother had asked God to forgive their sins through the sacrifice made by Jesus Christ on the cross.

Now, Lembui lived in a small village where all the people were related, sharing the family name of Murunga—but this village was just one small part of an immense region where nearly everyone shares that name. The region itself, in fact, is named Murunga's Family, and everyone's name ends in Murunga. Consequently, individual villages like Lembui's are close-knit, and the people treat one another's homes as their own—coming and going at will without awaiting an invitation or a special occasion. Needless to say, by sunrise everyone in the village knew that four strangers had arrived, and nearly everyone appeared at the hut door even while the roosters were still crowing.

The four men were on the point of collapse after a long day of mountain trekking followed by a sleepless night, so the villagers politely departed shortly after joining Lembui's family for breakfast. But over the course of the next two days, many of the villagers returned to hear their stories, as word had gone around that they had a great many fascinating tales. By the end of the week, Koinet and his friends found themselves at the center of a gathering, seated outside around a fire because the group was too large to cram into a hut. They told some stories from Scripture and listened as village elders told stories of their own, and the evening passed in an atmosphere of storytelling and laughter—but did not go beyond that point to discussing issues of eternity.

Lembui, however, more than made up for the apathy of his extended family. He spent each day herding his goats in the mountains and valleys, gone from before sunup till after sunset. Herding goats is not only a very lonely job, but it can also be quite dangerous—particularly in the mountains, which abound with natural hazards and wild predators, such as leopards—so goatherds frequently lead their flocks to common areas where the men can find human companionship while their herds graze. Each morning, Lembui would go out with eagerness, hurrying his flock as quickly as possible to one or another of the meeting grounds, for he was bursting with excitement to tell his friends what he had learned from the four men the night before. Each night, the men would tell him stories about God, and each day he would rehearse those stories for his fellow goatherds.

Two things resulted from this: Lembui grew very quickly in his understanding and wisdom concerning the Word of God, and half a dozen other goatherds asked Jesus to save them from sin. And that's not all: Lembui persuaded two of the village elders to join him in a Bible study in his home several nights per week. (None of them could read, but they had memorized the Bible stories they'd been hearing.) And Koinet and his friends found themselves with an open door into five other areas, for the goatherds who assembled together were from many different villages. This situation presented a new but welcome problem: the four men realized that they could not bring the gospel to the village as effectively as Lembui, since they were outsiders while he was a member of the family; however, Lembui couldn't read and thus could not hope to study the Bible without their help. So they decided to remain with Lembui and his mother for at least a month, studying the Bible together with the village elders and then traveling to the other villages to teach those goatherds who had accepted Christ. (And within the first month, six new churches were planted in the homes of ordinary men, uneducated goatherds from six different mountain tribes.)

As the days passed, however, Koinet grew increasingly restless, burning with desire to carry the gospel to his own family. At the end of his third week with Lembui, Koinet decided to separate from his companions, leaving them to minister to the growing churches while he continued on his original quest. He set out on his own the next morning, spending long days hiking through mountain and valley, seeking information from anyone he met, always heading northwest toward the border between two nations. Finally, after many days of searching, he found his family's encampment—a series of low earthen enclosures surrounded by a fence built of sharp thorny branches.

The tribe's welcome was far more gracious than Koinet had expected. After many years apart, his family members were excited to learn where he had gone and what he had done. The novelty of such a man walking unexpectedly into the encampment was itself sufficient to obliterate any sense of fear or old grudges, even if any of his former companions remembered such details of his youth—although few had forgotten his exploit in killing the lion. His older brother Simel was now one of the leaders of the clan, and Koinet was invited to share his little hut along with his three wives, fourteen children, and some goats.

Koinet spent the next two weeks telling his brother's family stories from the Bible, and they listened with rapt attention. He found, however, that nobody had much interest in the topics of sin or redemption, as these notions don't exist in animistic religions, and he was up against the same wall that he'd found in Lembui's village. Storytelling is a great way to spend the evening with the family, but it is not enough to open a person's eyes to the truth of God; there must be a sense that one is separated from God, and in animistic views everything is part of God—including oneself. (The truth is that no one can come to Christ without the work of the Holy Spirit, but Koinet was still learning to have faith in God's involvement with the gospel.)

Koinet was growing discouraged, but he continued to pray daily that the Lord would show Himself to his brother's family, demonstrating that He is God over all creation. Then one morning, Simel announced that he would be taking a group of men on a hunting trip. Koinet immediately volunteered, hoping to have some more time in close conversation with his brother. A group of twelve men left camp that afternoon, wrapped in brilliant scarlet robes and carrying their trademark oval shields and slender spears. Koinet was a very strong man, and he was in excellent condition after his weeks in the mountains, yet he found himself winded as he scrambled to keep up with the group in their rapid pace. It slowly dawned on him that this group was on a mission—though what it was he could not say—and their faces were set with purpose. The mountainous terrain to these men was like a paved road to an American, and they strode over the countryside without thought or effort. Before nightfall, they had reached the border with the neighboring nation, and they made camp on a cliffside that overlooked an open plain.

"Tomorrow night," said Simel, "we will gather what Enkai has given us." Koinet stood dumbfounded, for he finally understood his brother's true purpose for this trip: they were on a cattle raid. He was distraught at being associated with the expedition, but he also knew that his protests would do no good. He considered leaving the party and heading back to the village on his own, but nothing could be done until morning. He came to learn in future days that it is best to take the gospel to those who are open to hearing it—and his brother at this moment was not—but the Lord was at work all the same.

Koinet spent a sleepless night asking God for wisdom. "Lord," he prayed, "please stop my brother in his tracks. Do not let him proceed on this wicked plan. I am powerless, but you are all-powerful. Please intervene!"

The men arose early as one does when sleeping under the stars, but not because they had any pressing tasks for the daylight hours. Their plan—as Koinet came to understand it—was to wait until dusk, make their way to the plain below, liberate some cattle, and then to return homeward. Simel mentioned that the United Nations had an office on that plain, and Koinet wondered with a sick stomach whether some of those cattle were intended to assist refugees—the thousands of innocent people who were trying to flee the murder and mayhem that was ravaging the neighboring nation. But his brother would not listen to any pleas or arguments, and the group ate their breakfast with stony faces.

Koinet had no appetite, so he wandered a short distance away from the group and sat down in a shady grove to pray. (They were now on the outskirts of a mountain rainforest area, and trees grew in abundance.) "Lord," he cried silently, tears streaming down his cheeks, "I never intended this. I came here out of obedience to your Word, and now I am faced with nothing but evil choices. Please send me deliverance!" As he prayed, he could hear the distant sounds of the village on the plain below, as the little settlement started its workday. He heard some cattle mooing; he heard the horn of a truck, probably at the UN compound; he heard some yells of children playing. He heard the slightest hint of a rustle nearby. He looked up, expecting to see his brother. It wasn't his brother.

A long black figure was streaking toward him, and the air was rent with a hideous snarling scream. Koinet leaped to his feet, adrenaline pumping in his temples, as he recognized the form of a nearly six-foot-long black panther with yellow eyes narrowed and teeth laid bare racing low to the ground straight for him. In the space of a breath, the panther had leaped, great claws and teeth reaching for his throat. Koinet instinctively braced his legs and leaned slightly forward, raising his right arm across his chest to receive the animal's thrust (for he had neither shield nor spear). The cat threw its full 180 pounds against him, knocking him back a couple of paces—but Koinet stood his ground. For the briefest of moments, the two combatants stood facing one another like a pair of dancers, the cat standing upright with foreclaws sinking into Koinet's neck and shoulders, while snarling and glaring, as Koinet pushed with his arm against the creature's chest. The panther faced him eye-to-eye, and what he saw in that baleful stare was raw slavering lust— whether for his blood or his soul, Koinet could not be sure.

All of this takes far longer to read than it took to happen; it was a matter of two heartbeats from sighting to fighting, and there was no time for thought or action. Koinet reacted with instinct: he cried out to God.

"In Jesus' name!" he shouted. "In Jesus' name! I bind you! I bind you!"

You might think it strange to be attacked by a panther without warning and to respond by shouting in its face, but stranger things happened next. The panther withdrew the claws that were rending Koinet's neck; then it actually pushed him back a step with its immense paws, causing itself to stand fully upright in the process—its eyes glazing over and saliva drooling from its lower jaw. Then it dropped unceremoniously to the ground and lay calmly down on its belly.

The other men came racing into the grove in response to the commotion, spears and shields in position, faces set with grim ferocity. Then they all stopped short, and their fierceness turned to fear. Ordinarily, a large cat like a panther—or even a lion—would be no match for a dozen Maasai warriors and their spears. But there was something so singular and strange in this confrontation, something about this feline that was far from ordinary, that the men were gripped with terror. Even Koinet, who had once slain a lion single-handed, was frozen to the spot where the animal had shoved him, trembling with a horror that did not come solely from the sudden attack. There was a sense of evil about this creature that seemed to transcend the physical realm, and the entire group felt its malice.

And immediately, the entire group gave in to the fear, the eleven dropping their weapons and fleeing the grove, leaving Koinet to stand alone with the resting cat. Even his own brother had abandoned him, and he was left only with the conviction that God was still there with him.

The others scattered into the surrounding wilderness, some heading toward a valley to the south, some throwing themselves under bushes, and three (including Simel) charging blindly down the narrow path to the plain below. These three ran past the cattle they'd come to steal, as Simel led them toward the UN compound to find aid from their intended victims. Some women screamed; children fled at their approach, and two men emerged from the compound carrying AK-47s. One can hardly blame them; the sight of three Maasai warriors charging down from the mountain would be enough to frighten anyone, and their yells and shouts sounded like battle cries to the people they passed. The armed men quickly understood the situation, however, from Simel's breathless bursts of facts—"Panther . . . man-eater . . . attack . . . my brother" coming between gasps for air—and in short order a Land Rover roared up the mountain trail carrying ten armed men.

The group arrived to find Koinet still standing where they'd left him nearly an hour before, with the panther lying quietly near his feet. The men clambered out of the vehicle and rushed toward the grove—but they did not fire their high-powered assault rifles. Indeed, they did not even come within shooting distance, for the same fear gripped them all: black and white, native and foreign, educated and illiterate, none were immune, and all fell back in dismay.

Simel plucked up what little courage remained. "Koinet," he called through cupped hands, "if you are not eaten, please come out!"

Oddly enough, this comment broke Koinet's paralysis, and he started to laugh at its absurdity. Then he laughed at the panther that he had so recently feared, now lying in submission before him, only the tip of its tail twitching back and forth, suggesting that the animal was not happy about the situation. Then he laughed louder still at his own preposterous fear. He'd been as immobilized as the cat was now, but unlike the cat *he'd* had a choice in the matter. He realized that he had allowed his enemy to use his most common weapon against him, freezing him with fear—and fear is the enemy of God's people, for a man who submits to it will stop submitting to God. He laughed again until the tears rolled down for the second time that morning, and he couldn't resist having some fun at the expense of his foe. Without the slightest anxiety, he walked up to the panther and tickled its ribs.

The animal blinked, relaxed, and opened its mouth in a gaping yawn. Without looking at Koinet, it rolled onto its side, curled up, and went to sleep with one paw folded over its brow.

The UN workers took Koinet back down to their compound to dress his claw wounds, with Simel and about half of his hunting party crammed inside the Land Rover or sitting on the roof. (The other brave warriors had not stopped running yet.) The men spent most of the day at the compound, eating their host's food, asking for medicines for their children, accepting gifts of blankets and sandals, and remaining stubbornly oblivious to their own hypocrisy. Around six o'clock, they made their way back up the mountain path to their encampment.

And there they found the remainder of their friends huddled together behind their shields, literally trembling with fear. "The panther!" they hissed as Koinet's group approached, furious gestures coupled with insistent commands to be silent. "The panther—it is still there!"

"No," exclaimed Simel, too loudly for the comfort of his friends. "No—how can it be?"

"Perhaps it is dead," Koinet suggested, as much to bolster his own confidence as anything. The group quietly and hesitantly made their way to the grove, peeking from behind trees and squatting themselves in hopes of becoming invisible. There it was, the giant brute still curled up as it was when Koinet last saw it.

"Yes," Simel said slowly (and quietly), "yes . . . it must be dead."

Then Koinet understood. "No," he said in a loud voice that made the others jump and shoosh him. "No! It is not dead. It is staying there because I commanded it to."

Simel couldn't restrain a loud guffaw. "Because you told it to? The black panther is sleeping quietly because you *told it to*?" Some of his friends joined him in laughter—more quietly, however.

"Yes, my brother, because I told it to—in Jesus' name. I *commanded* the creature in the name of Jesus, and it had to submit."

"So now, my brother, now you have become an animal shaman? What will be next—charming snakes from baskets in the marketplace?"

"No, Simel, it was not my power, it was the power of my God. He is the One who created all things, including that animal, and His creatures are under His authority—whether they want to be or not."

"It sounds to me like your God is at *your* beck and call. All you do is say 'I command,' and your God must obey."

"No, it is not like that. Jesus said in His Word that if we—"

"You and your Jesus!" Simel interrupted in a rage, no longer afraid of waking the beast. "I'm tired of hearing about your Jesus. If your Jesus is so powerful, have Him chase away the panther!"

"If He does, will you believe?"

"Ha! That will happen, I'm sure!" Simel looked around on the others, as if for support. Receiving none, he added in bravado, "Of course I will!"

Koinet looked steadfastly in his brother's face. "I mean this, Simel. You must decide—today. This is no game, my brother. Will you believe?"

Simel's mocking rant subsided, and he became grave. "My brother," he said, drawing himself upright, "if your Jesus froze this panther, then your Jesus can chase it away. If He does that, then I will believe."

Koinet no longer feared the beast, and he marched up to it with boldness, pushed it with his foot, and cried in a loud voice, "In Jesus' name—you there; panther—in Jesus' name now, *go away!*"

The black cat rose gracefully to its feet and arched its back, stretching its giant paws to the front and digging the claws deep into the soil. Then, with upcurved tail, it rolled forward onto its front paws and stretched its hind legs straight back, first one, then the other, extending more vicious claws in the process. It all but purred as it gaped its mouth and curled its tongue in a luxurious yawn, as though it were the most docile, if overgrown, domestic pet. But it turned jaundiced eyes to meet Koinet's in a malignant glare that brought goose bumps to his arms. As it moved nonchalantly away, its eyes moving to and fro in search of more prey, Koinet noticed for the first time an old scabbed wound atop its head, as from a crushing blow that would never heal.

He turned back to see an even more amazing sight: his elder brother collapsing to his knees with great sobs, pulling up clods of grass and matting them against the top of his head. Koinet rushed over and pulled him to his feet, himself in tears now. That very evening he prayed with his brother—indeed, with all eleven men—and they surrendered to Jesus as their Savior. That night, as the group sat around the fire, Koinet explained the Word of God. He told them about David and Samson, men who had slain lions through the power of God. (He did not mention his own youthful conquest, for it no longer had meaning.) He told them the truth of creation and the origin of death in the world. And he explained how Jesus came to be the Last Adam, offering mankind a chance to be born again into God's eternal family.

In later days, God used Simel in dramatic ways for His kingdom, but those stories will have to wait for another book.

CHAPTER 8

THE DISCOVERY PROCESS

No one can come to Me unless the Father who sent
Me draws him; and I will raise him up at the last day. It
is written in the prophets, "And they shall all be taught
by God." Therefore everyone who has heard and
learned from the Father comes to Me. (John 6:44–45)

In our modern-day methodology, we have been wrongly
taught that we are to approach a lost person, present a
propositional statement, and ask the person to confess
his faith by repeating a formulaic prayer after us—and
then we pronounce him to be a Christian. In this
chapter, we see how Dawit allowed the Father to *draw*
people unto Himself and teach them from His Word
about Jesus His Son. It is vitally important that we follow the leading of the Holy Spirit and allow the Father
in heaven to do His work in the hearts of men. We see
it first with Dawit working with Guma, and later with
Guma working with Quadir.

During these weeks and months, Dawit had been busy seeking out men and women who seemed open to hearing about
God's role in their lives, people whom Jesus called "sons of peace"

(Luke 10). The Lord had used Dawit to lead many to Himself and to plant more than a dozen churches in homes scattered throughout a wide geographical area. He and Tamrat, his partner in ministry, worked very closely together, traveling to towns and villages with the gospel for a period, followed by a period spent at home with their families. After a time, the two men felt led to revisit some of the churches they'd planted to exhort and encourage the new believers—a process that actually brought at least as much encouragement to Dawit and Tamrat as to their new brothers and sisters in Christ.

They decided that it would be expedient to hire a driver for a few days since their itinerary was far-flung, so Dawit found a man named Guma who agreed to carry them wherever they needed to go. Guma owned an eye-catching bit of African public transportation in the form of a homemade donkey cart. He had collected an axle and wheel assembly (complete with leaf springs and Dunlop tires) from a wrecked car, some fenders and bumpers from various other motor vehicles, numerous iron rods and rusty bolts, a few pieces of lattice, an old mattress, and two dead trees; then he had fashioned the random materials into a very serviceable carriage, pulled by his pet donkey named Ears. The contraption sported a harlequin array of colors: patches of crimson mottled with brilliant sapphire and cadmium yellow, all tastefully muted in a patina of rust and capped off by a dazzling orange vinyl tarp for a roof. It looked like something off the pages of Dr. Seuss, and it was Guma's pride and joy.

Dawit and Tamrat spent a great deal of time in that cart over the next three days, trying to visit as many believers as possible between dawn and midnight each day. This made Guma quite literally a captive audience, and the Christians did not waste the opportunity to share God's Word with him. They liked their cab driver immediately. He was a diminutive man with a gentle demeanor, yet it didn't take them long to discover that he and his donkey shared some traits in common. He would patiently listen to all they said about Jesus, then quietly try to refute their arguments, contradict their observations, and ask them loaded questions—all the time smiling gently and asking his donkey for corroboration.

"We are traveling to visit people who are Christians like us," Dawit had told him on their first day. "We have devoted our lives to serving God—and we're very pleased to have you serving us in that process!"

"That is good to know," Guma replied in his soft voice. "I try to serve the gods every day by treating the world around me with deep respect—isn't that right, Ears?"

"There is only one God," Dawit clarified, though he suspected that his cab driver had deliberately misunderstood.

"Oh, god is in everything, even in old Ears here."

"Well, it is true that God *created* everything," said Dawit, "but He exists *apart* from everything at the same time."

"Uh-oh," Guma said with an endearing pout. "Did you hear that, Ears? You're not god after all. Please don't be sad, though; I still love you." He gave a slight twitch to the reigns, to which the donkey brayed as if on cue.

Guma had grown up in a family that believed in the religion of intellect; one could only discover truth through reason and investigation. He was what many in the West would call a skeptic, and he had an ingrained habit of questioning everything. There was no such thing as a miracle; he would argue that everything has a perfectly rational explanation in accordance with the laws of nature. Yet Guma was an honest skeptic (two traits that rarely appear together), and acknowledged that there must be a

God who could be known by mankind, at least to some degree; this led him to begin investigating world religions when he grew to manhood. He had begun studying the Qur'an with a local sheikh and had been enthusiastically encouraged to become a sheikh himself, but he had eventually become disillusioned with its presupposition that a man can become holy simply by observing a system of religious activities—rigid and complex as they might be. At the time he met Dawit and Tamrat, Guma was exploring the belief systems of animism—and was already rejecting them as absurd. The problem was that he had nothing else to investigate next. Having rejected every teaching he'd encountered, he was well along the road to bitter cynicism.

Nevertheless, he enjoyed his conversations with his two passengers—although he took care not to let them know it. They were never aggressive with their gospel talk, and would only discuss theology when he initiated it. Whenever he grew frustrated with his inability to stymie them with tricky questions, he would simply deflect the conversation onto some mundane topic (usually by appealing to Ears), and the two men would let the gospel wait. By the third day, however, his deeper interest was fully aroused. He sensed that there might actually be some true answers to his questions about God, and he feared that he might lose the chance of learning those answers when the men returned home. On their final journey, he suddenly steered the cart off the road, loosened the reigns, and turned a very serious face to his passengers.

"Look," he challenged, "what do you guys get from all this? I mean, you have been traveling all over the countryside, spending money on a cart—but what do *you* get out of it? You gather people everywhere we go; you preach to them and teach them—I don't understand what you're gaining."

"We want to bring many people to the kingdom of God," Dawit explained.

"Yes, so you keep saying. But here's a question I have: before you can bring others to the kingdom of God, are you sure that *you're* in the kingdom of God?" Dawit opened his mouth to answer, but Guma had breached a floodgate and now the questions poured out.

"And who's to say that anyone can *get* into God's kingdom in the first place? Yes, I know you say that people can inherit the kingdom of God, and you travel about proclaiming this—but how can you be sure it's true? And another thing: How can you be so sure that the people you're preaching to don't have access to the kingdom of God some other way? Who are you to go around the countryside telling everyone that you have this secret?

"You've told me, 'Jesus saves us, Jesus saves us'—you, *you* have told me this—but you yourself will die like everybody else! There is no difference. You are nice guys, and I like talking to you, but I don't see how this is different from any other religion. Everybody claims they know the truth about God, some guys this way and some guys that way, but in the end everybody dies the same death. So what makes you so sure and so bold?"

Dawit was a bit overwhelmed by the torrent of questions, but Tamrat quietly drew out his Bible and opened to the gospel of John.

"Here is what Jesus said: 'I am the way, the truth, and the life. No one comes to the Father except through Me.' He also said this," Tamrat continued, flipping back a few pages. "'Most assuredly, I say to you, unless one is born again, he cannot see the kingdom of God.' And this: 'For God so loved the world that He gave His only begotten Son, that whoever believes in Him should not perish but have everlasting life.'"[12]

Tamrat showed him many more such passages that state emphatically that no man can escape physical death but that there is a second death that anyone *can* escape—but only through one means: the blood shed by Jesus Christ on the cross. Guma listened intently, for once his skeptical counter-questions disarmed, but his brow remained clouded.

"I am not convinced," he announced after some time. He turned his face to the front, gave the reigns a shake, and coaxed Ears into motion.

"It is a dangerous business to remain stubbornly unconvinced, my friend," Dawit said gently after they had regained the road. "You have heard the truth; now what will you do with it?"

"I will tell you," Guma said softly after a pause. "This God who has revealed it to you—let Him reveal it to *me* also!"

"He *has* revealed it to you—in His written Word. No man has the right to demand more."

Guma glanced at the men, his mouth set in a tight line. "Alright, fair enough. Then I will read this 'written Word' for myself. I *can* read, you know," he added, just a trifle defensively (for nearly half the adults in this nation cannot). "I am no ordinary cart driver."

They trundled along in silence for a few moments, then Guma turned a softened face to his friends. "If you will give me a Bible, I will read it. I will do more than just read it: I will evaluate my life according to it, and see what I find."

His passengers beamed with joy as they handed him a Bible in Amharic. "That is the only way to read the Bible," Tamrat added.

"Yes, yes . . . I knew you would say that," Guma said, his normal banter returning. Then he added, "So I will study your book, and who knows: maybe one day I will come to have faith."

He gave the reigns another shake. "That would be a *real* miracle, now wouldn't it, Ears?"

The next day, Guma began reading the Bible—and he read it voraciously. He would read it in the darkness of morning prior to hitching Ears to the cart; he'd read it while sitting in town waiting for passengers; he'd read it while driving passengers; he'd read it when the passengers got out. He read it at lunch, and he read it after supper; he read it until the cover fell off—and still he had questions. Some days he would see Dawit, since his village was near Guma's town, and the two would ride together on their way somewhere (and frequently nowhere) talking about what Guma had read. Dawit would answer his questions as best he could. Sometimes the answers were unknowable; sometimes they were quickly found in the Scriptures—but always they were unsatisfactory to Guma. This went on for four months, and then Guma had a dream.

He found himself standing by the side of the road in his town, all alone with nothing stirring. A slight breeze came up wafting a sweet fragrance, and he heard footsteps. He turned to see Dawit approaching, carrying something that seemed to glow. No words were spoken; Dawit simply came to him and unfurled a beautiful white cape with a hood. He placed the hood atop Guma's head, then walked around him to smooth it out and drape it across his shoulders and down his back. Then he continued on his way and left Guma alone again.

A voice spoke, but Guma did not understand what it said. He looked around but saw nobody, even though he could see more clearly from the light emitted by his new cape. He rubbed the cloth between his fingers—so light and soft, yet durable, made of some fabric that he'd never encountered before. Clearly this was a precious gift.

"Do I need to pay someone for this cape?" he asked, hoping that the unseen visitor might speak again.

"Ah, good—I am glad you've asked that," spoke the voice. "You do not need to pay for it. Indeed, you could not if it were demanded. Just receive it; it is a free gift from me. Accept it."

Guma was both relieved and embarrassed by these words. He fondled the cape again, wrestling with emotion. "Why would you want to give me an expensive gift? I don't even know who you are."

"Why do you argue?" the voice asked. "Please just follow what I reveal to you. The cape is free, but it brings responsibilities with it; all gifts do. You need to go to the person who gave you this cape, and I will show you what to do next."

"But I'm just a cart driver. Why do you—"

"Yes, you *were* just a cart driver. But from now on, you will no longer be just a cart driver; you will be a soul winner. You are going to win many souls to me. For this reason, do not argue with me; just come and follow me, and obey what I reveal to you."

"But I don't have any work, I don't have any money," Guma responded immediately. He was thrilled with his new cape and wanted to keep it, yet somehow it made him feel humble and dependent upon someone—and this clouded his joy.

"A moment ago, you wanted to pay for the cape," the voice answered. "Now you have no money and no work. You must make a decision: keep the cape or give it back."

"But if I leave my work, my cart . . . if I go find this man . . . plus, I might not even be *able* to find him! Yes, that could be a big problem—I don't know where he lives, you see." But the voice remained silent. "I want the cape," he continued in desperation, "thank you, I like it—but what you ask! What am I to do? How will I feed my children? I am a cart driver!"

"You argue with me!" the voice said sternly. "Let me show you something. How does a cart driver work when he cannot move?"

Suddenly, Guma felt his legs tighten uncontrollably in the worst muscle spasm he'd ever felt. It hurt like fire for a moment, then all went numb from the waist down. He rubbed his thighs, but there was no sensation in them—he could not even feel the pressure of his hands. He tried to sit down but his legs did not cooperate, and he fell on his back in the grass. He tried to stand, but could not move his legs. Then he cried out in anguish.

"I surrender! I yield to you! Please, Lord, make me walk again. Save me from this paralysis! Please heal me, and I'll go wherever you are sending me. Please: give me your mercy."

"My son," the voice said gently, "you have been paralyzed for a long time, you just didn't know it. I want to remove *all* your paralysis, but you must submit to me first. Will you go to the place that I will show you?"

"Yes."

The voice asked again, "Will you go to the place that I will show you?"

Again, Guma responded, "Yes."

The voice asked the question a third time: "Will you go to the place that I will show you?"

This time Guma's stubborn pride collapsed. "Yes, Lord, yes! I want to obey you; I want to know the truth. Please: I will argue no longer. I will obey."

"Then stand up!" the voice commanded, and Guma leaped to his feet, running in place and lifting his knees as high as they'd go, rejoicing in his vigor.

"Do you understand my power and authority?"

"Yes, Lord, now I understand. Your words have both: power *and* authority."

"And now you will obey my words?"

"Yes, Lord—now I will obey completely."

He suddenly felt hands touching him, caressing him, and he realized that he'd been arrayed in a new set of clothes—tunic and robes and sandals that all glowed with the brilliance of the cape.

Then he awoke. His first thought was, "Am I paralyzed? Let me check." He moved his feet and legs underneath his blanket, and his wife stirred beside him—nothing was amiss. He lay awake for the dawn, pondering his strange dream. That morning, he and Ears rattled off in their cart as usual, but they did not take up their ordinary stand near the marketplace. Instead, Guma continued through town and headed toward Dawit's village, bouncing along the tracks and trails until he found his house.

"Okay," Guma said when he'd found his friend, "I am ready to have faith now." He explained to Dawit about his dream, and the two men spent the morning in prayer and Bible reading. At noon, Guma had to return to his post in the town, for he could not afford missing an entire day of work.

As he climbed into the seat of his cart, he turned back to Dawit with a mischievous look. "It's not because I've come to know some deep secret or understand some dark mystery, you know." He flicked the reigns. "I just don't want to get paralyzed. Right, Ears?"

Like most new Christians, Guma had to learn how to channel his zeal for the gospel. At first, he shared the news of salvation wantonly and aggressively, taking advantage of his passengers' captive status as they rode along. After a few responses of, "Shut up and drive," he realized that some people simply were not interested in hearing the good news. Gradually, he learned to find bridges in conversation that would permit his passengers to indicate an interest; if they had one, he would gently lead into discussing the salvation of Christ; if not, he would not press the matter.

One important thing grew out of this process: Guma began keeping a prayer journal. It started when one woman broke down in tears pouring out a tale of misery and despair when he asked her why she looked so angry that morning. She did not want to hear about God that day, but Guma promised that he would pray for her sad situation, and that very day he purchased a notebook and wrote down her name and needs. He carried the journal with him wherever he went, and he soon became known as "the praying cartman." It wasn't long before people would wait in the marketplace in hopes of catching a ride with him (and he carried five or six at a time) just to share prayer requests, and many would return later to tell him how his prayers were answered—all of which he dutifully logged into the journal. (I have seen this journal, and it contained more than nine hundred requests and answers at the time.)

One night, the Lord appeared to Guma in a dream, telling him to go visit a man in his town named Quadir and to give him a message. Now, this man was a renowned thug, a thief and bully who ran a small gang and was notorious for a violent and unpredictable temper—and Guma was understandably afraid. "What if he robs me?" he thought as he lay in his bed. "How will I feed my family? Why, forget *rob* me—what if he *kills* me? Who will look after my children then?"

These fears were well grounded; for Quadir had built his reputation on an almost mythical encounter he'd had as a younger man. The story held that he'd single-handedly confronted a gang of thirty men in Yappa once, killing the leader and his lieutenant, crippling another, and putting the rest to flight. It didn't matter how much truth may have been in this story; for the people in Guma's town had enough of their own stories to supplement it: tales of extortion, robbery, murder, and so forth, all told with a mixture of fear and awe. Guma rehearsed a few of these grisly tales as his wife slept, but in the end he steeled himself to obey God's command, leaving the consequences in His hands. "If he kills me," he told himself as he dressed, "then let him kill me. It is God who has commanded this."

Early in the morning, he and Ears bypassed their usual spot in the marketplace and continued across town to the well-known headquarters of Quadir's gang—and Guma was frankly disappointed to discover that Quadir was there. He was seated in a decrepit wooden chair smoking a fat cigar, his long legs stretched in front of him, with several henchmen slouching nearby chewing khat. His broad shoulders and thick arms lent some credence to the tales of his violence, and Guma stood frozen in the doorway. Quadir slowly turned his face toward him, squinting through the blue smoke that filled the little concrete room.

"What do you want, little man?" he asked in the voice of a bull.

"I have come—" Guma began in a tremulous voice.

"What? Speak up or get out, fool!" Quadir roared. His thugs smiled, anticipating some entertainment.

Guma cleared his throat, attempting to look bold. "I have come," he repeated, unconsciously taking the stern tone that he used when his children misbehaved (which didn't intimidate the children either), "I have come with a message from God. For you." He could feel his bravado slipping away. "That is—I mean—if you are Mr. Quadir."

The big man made a wry face as he took the cigar from his mouth. "And who exactly are you, little man?"

"My name is Guma, and I come with—"

"Ah! The praying cartman!" The gangster's greasy face beamed with amusement as derisive laughter burst from his gang. "So, you have been praying for *me*, have you?"

"Well," Guma answered sheepishly, "not exactly." Quadir was in a rare good humor that morning, having satisfied himself the night before in a variety of carnal pleasures, and he took an immediate fancy to the quiet little man who stood trembling in the doorway. Inviting him to come closer (much to Guma's discomfort), he leaned forward on the arm of his chair and peered intently into his face.

"Now . . . what is this you came to say?"

And in that moment, Guma suddenly felt himself enveloped in peace, as though he had donned a cloak of invincibility. He realized that this man, powerful though he might be, could do nothing whatsoever to him without the permission of the God who had sent him. And this conviction filled him with a boldness that was not bravado.

"Almighty God has sent me," he declared in a voice that made the walls ring. "He has commanded me, and I have come!"

The sudden authority of these words wiped the smugness from Quadir's face. He sat up astonished and gazed at the small man with a new respect. "And why would this God send you to me?"

"This is what God told me to say to you: you need to come to Jesus immediately!" A collective gasp from the henchmen caused Guma to pause, but Quadir sat staring at him without expression. "If you don't receive Him, the Lord told me that you will spear a person, and you will end up in prison. All your friends will desert you, and you will be in chains."

Guma fully expected a violent outburst from the villain before him, but it was his turn to be astonished at the man's reaction. For Quadir slumped in his chair as though the wind had gone out of him; his face turned white, and his hands became unsteady—for the fear of the Lord had descended upon his soul.

"I believe you," he said in a thin voice. "I believe this is from God—for how else could you have known my thoughts?" He glanced almost fearfully at the men around him, who had stepped back against the walls at their leader's uncharacteristic behavior; then he hardened his expression.

"How can I turn to worshipping this Jesus?" he asked petulantly. "I am a Muslim, and I would be killed as an infidel if I did that."

"But you are going to prison if you don't," Guma exclaimed.

"Better alive in prison than dead in the streets," the man said emphatically. "I might as well die for killing, if I am to die for this Jesus."

"Don't be a fool!" Guma commanded. (He would later marvel at his unthinking boldness.) "You have it backwards. Better to die for Jesus than to perish as a murderer." The henchmen, all but forgotten, made some growling sounds at these words. But Guma was not to be stopped. "Do you think I came here for fun? I feared for my own life! Your reputation, you know . . . But to suffer for obedience is far nobler than to suffer for cowardice."

The men standing around were amazed at such an accusation: he, the great Quadir—a coward! They awaited a storm, but it did not come. Instead, the fearsome man looked about him as though he were trapped, gripping his shirtfront with both hands. Then, as if in sudden desperation, he snatched a fistful of khat from a table beside him and shoved it into his mouth.

"My family would kill me," he said thickly. "I would become an infidel—and *this* is worse than being a murderer, little man!"

Guma tried to press upon him the urgency of the situation, but the khat had numbed and emboldened him. He did not reject the message, but neither would he be persuaded to act upon it. Instead, he said Guma should come back in a couple of days. In that time he would work it out, and then he'd be ready to receive Jesus.

But in a couple of days, Guma was put off again. Quadir flooded him with questions, a few that were pertinent and many that were mere stalling. "You have frightened me," he said, "but I am not convinced just the same. Come back in a few days and we will talk further."

On his next visit, Quadir did not permit him to enter the shack, but sent a henchman with another appointment. Come back in a few days, he was told, and Quadir will see you. He has many questions that must be answered first.

After this third dismissal, Guma decided to intercede between Quadir and his family. A few discreet questions led him to the home of Quadir's father, Munib. He found the elderly man lying on a pallet at the rear of his hut under layers of old blankets, a cripple who had not risen from his bed in more than five years. Guma sat by his side and quietly explained the situation to him, to all of which the old man simply nodded without surprise.

After a short silence, the man looked at Guma. "Why do you come to me?" he asked. "My son has grown into a violent man; that I know full well. But what am I to do? Why come to me if he won't see you?"

"Because God is going to make him perish. Please: permit him to come to Jesus. It is all you can do, but it is more than enough. Otherwise, he is going to die by God's hand."

"If my son will truly be saved, rescued from this course—if he will become a good person . . ." The old man turned his face to the wall with a sigh. "Take him. Let him be a Christian."

Guma drove his cart as fast as old Ears could manage back to Quadir's house to share the news, but he was met at the door once again by one of Quadir's lieutenants. "Do not keep coming here," he said menacingly. "He says to come next week, so come next week."

The next night, the Lord again visited Guma in a dream. "Time is running out for Quadir," the Lord told him. "If he does not submit to me within the week, he will kill somebody, and he will be arrested. Tell him this again."

That morning Guma phoned Dawit and asked him to come with Tamrat, and two days later the three men went to see Quadir one last time.

"You have brought friends, I see," Quadir said as they entered. He was seated in his chair, this time alone, and he was looking haggard.

"I brought them as witnesses, Mr. Gangster," Guma said forcefully. "I want you to know that, if you do not listen to what God has said, your blood will be upon your own head—and these men will bear testimony of this."

Quadir was visibly shaken by these strong words, and he stared blankly at Guma—the "little man" who had trembled in his presence not long before.

"Listen to me now," Guma continued. "God has told me this thing again: if you don't accept Jesus right now, He showed me that you're going to kill a peaceful person. And as a result of that you will end up bound in prison chains."

Without waiting for a reply, Guma turned on his heel, and the three men left. That very night, Quadir got himself intoxicated with liquor and khat, and he put into action a plan that he'd concocted some time earlier. He went with two of his henchmen to the home of a merchant who had cheated him; they stood outside his door and called him out; and when he appeared, Quadir drove a spear through his belly.

The following Monday, Guma and Dawit spent the morning at a courthouse in the next town in order to be present for Quadir's arraignment. Contrary to all expectation, Quadir stood before the judge in chains and confessed his guilt in murdering the innocent man. It may have been one of the speediest trials in the modern world, and the judge sentenced him to twenty years in prison. As he was escorted from the courtroom, he noticed Guma and was permitted to speak with him.

"God came to me through you," Quadir said, his face drawn and pale, "but I did not use the opportunity. I have ruined my life, but I want my brothers to accept Jesus. I will send them a letter when I can. Please: you go visit them for me. I want them to hear."

So Dawit and Guma made a detour on their way home to visit Quadir's father. They found him on his pallet, being tended by Quadir's younger sister named Tawbah, who had walked thirty miles to be with her family when she learned of her brother's arrest.

"I know why you have come," said the old man, trying to sit up with Tawbah's help.

Guma began to rehearse the story of his attempts to warn Quadir, but Munib interrupted him. "I know. What have I to do here but think and pray for my son? I know that God gave him many chances to turn away." He paused as Tawbah wiped some sweat from his forehead. "My son has been an example to us all, I'm afraid—a very bad example. And now here you are, come to *me* and my family with the same message: turn to God while you can. I have been speaking with my daughter since she arrived, and we are of the same mind on this. Our Islam has not helped us; maybe your Christianity can."

Tawbah returned to her own family a few days later, but Guma and Dawit continued to visit Munib once a week for the following year.

"We would each lay a hand on one of his legs," Guma would cheerfully tell his passengers, "and gradually, very slowly, he began to walk again. Sort of 'step by step,' right Ears?"

CHAPTER 9

THE GREAT COMMISSION

And Jesus came and spoke to them, saying, "All authority has been given to Me in heaven and on earth. Go therefore and make disciples of all the nations, baptizing them in the name of the Father and of the Son and of the Holy Spirit, teaching them to observe all things that I have commanded you; and lo, I am with you always, even to the end of the age." (Matthew 28:18–20)

The Great Commission reflects the heart of God the Father, who did not spare His own Son, but sent Him to be a messenger to a hostile world to communicate the truth of God. So then, how can we refuse to obey when God asks us to go to the nations and make disciples—especially when He says that He will be with us? Sometimes, like Jirani, we have to be prompted by someone else to go, but remember the story that Jesus told about the ninety-nine sheep: only one was missing, but Jesus went to find it (Luke 15:1–7). How many are missing because someone didn't go?

Time passed, and Jirani had grown into manhood while working with his adopted Swedish father. He had also taken a wife, a childhood sweetheart named Hadhi from his hometown, and the two had moved to Yappa. A growing church in that city had invited Jirani to come work with them, and Oskar and Lisa sent the couple off with blessings and sadness.

One Sunday afternoon, Hadhi was sweeping the main sanctuary of the church while Jirani finished some paperwork in an anteroom. She was humming a hymn to herself when she heard a footstep behind her; she turned and barely suppressed a scream to find a man standing almost against her heels. He wore a long black beard and white robes with a Muslim skull cap on his head, and his eyes had the gleam of a zealot. Seeing her alarm, however, he held up a hand to calm her.

"I want to speak with you," he said without a smile.

Hadhi felt her knees trembling, but she answered boldly, "What do you want?"

"I just want to talk to you," he said again.

Hadhi recognized that this man was a sheikh, and she feared that he had come to cause trouble. "No," she said, drawing herself up, "it is better if you speak with my husband." Without waiting for a response, she called Jirani, and he came quickly at the tone of urgency in her voice.

"What can I do for you?" he asked.

"My name is Amin, and I am a follower of Isa," the man answered in a loud voice—for it was none other than the sheikh who had taken the young boys to Yappa in hopes of sending them to Mecca. He had become a follower of Isa al Masih, and had moved to Yappa permanently in order to carry the gospel to the former members of his mentor's mosque. "I used to be a sheikh, and I came here because of the name of your church."

"The name of my church?" Jirani responded hesitantly. "What name of my church?"

"Gospel Church for the World!" Amin's voice rang through the sanctuary. "You do not know the name of your own church?"

"No, I just meant . . . I mean . . ." Jirani was flustered by the man's commanding presence and aggressiveness. "Why is this important to you?"

"I have never heard such a name for a church in Africa, so I am surprised to find it here. How long since you started this church?"

Jirani collected his thoughts, trying to understand where this conversation was leading. "Ah . . . we've been a church for . . . four years now."

"Four years!" Amin stepped back in surprise. "Four years—and how far did you go in those four years?"

"How far did we go?"

"Yes! Calling yourself 'Gospel Church for the World'—how far did you go?"

Jirani felt like a man in a blindfold, trying to feel his way along. "No," he hesitated, "no . . . we are just here in Yappa. We didn't go anywhere."

Amin's face became even more grave. "Ohhh . . . ," he said, shaking his beard, "that is not good." He squinted one eye at Jirani. "You must go. You must do according to your vision."

"My vision?"

"Yes," he bellowed. "Your vision! If you got a vision from the Lord to go to the whole world, to carry His gospel to all peoples—well, you should not have stayed *here* for four years!"

Jirani just stared in response.

"I have come, then, to take you to the world—to help you do your vision for all people."

Now, it happened that Jirani and Hadhi had been praying for several months for the Lord to open a door of ministry in Yappa. They knew that He had called them to minister at this church, but so far they had not found a particular *way* to minister. So at Amin's words, the couple exchanged glances.

"Is this true? Has the Lord sent you to take us to ministry?" Amin simply folded his arms and glared. "But *where* will you take us?"

"I will take you to the Muslims, that's where. We will go to a place where *I* have been called—but I need help—and *you* are that help." Amin sensed that the young couple wanted to serve the Lord wherever they were called, and he suddenly relaxed into a broad grin. The three sat down together while Amin explained a vision he'd had concerning a Muslim town some distance from Yappa. He'd visited there several times himself, but for various reasons he could not do the work alone. One of those reasons was that Amin did not speak the tribal dialect, and his success had been limited when speaking Amharic. (He hadn't known of Jirani's linguistic skills when he entered that church. In fact he had known nothing whatsoever and had gone in almost on a whim, but the meeting was not a coincidence.)

After listening for a time, Jirani felt a mixture of excitement and fear. "But, you know," he said, "it is not easy to go to Muslims and preach the gospel. It's definitely not easy! No church in our region has tried this, in fact." He looked at Hadhi, noting the same mixture of emotions on her face. "Please: give us time to pray about it."

Amin slowly nodded. "Okay," he assented. "How long do you want to pray? And please: do *not* say four years more!"

"No," the couple laughed, "not four years. Just let us pray for one month, then we will tell you."

Amin abruptly rose to leave. "Oh, and one more thing," he stopped to add. "Your church: it is called Gospel Church for the World. Just so you know if someone else asks."

One month later, the four of them (for Amin's wife had joined him in the Lord's work) spent a day on public buses, followed by a morning in a hired minibus in order to reach the large village where they were expected. They crested a ridge to discover a large group of people—some fifty men and women—waiting for them underneath a tree. The men were wearing *kurtas* (knee-length tunics) over baggy pants that resembled hospital scrubs and prayer shawls draped over their shoulders; the women wore full-length gowns of muted reds and browns, their heads covered with scarves. But Jirani was not looking at their clothing; what he saw immediately was that all the men were carrying spears. These were not the long, sinewy spears of the Maasai, but short throwing spears with tapered steel blades—very businesslike and very deadly.

Amin noticed his expression. "Do not be alarmed," he said. "It is a tribal custom to carry spears. They carry them wherever they go, except into larger towns where they are not allowed. They mean you no harm."

Jirani was not entirely convinced, as the people were watching them climb out of the minibus with stony faces, and he walked quickly to get in front of his wife. They tentatively approached the tree; then the two groups stood staring at one another, nobody moving or speaking.

"What am I going to do now?" Jirani demanded in a stage whisper.

"Look," said Amin, pointing his beard in the direction of the crowd. "They have spears—but you have a Bible. Teach them about the Creator God who sent His Son!"

"But will they listen?"

"Of course they will listen! That is why they are waiting here."

Jirani still was not convinced. "How can people holding spears want to listen to me?" Nevertheless, he opened his Bible to John 1 and began to read in a loud voice, translating the Amharic text into the tribal dialect as he went. He told the people that Jesus is the only way to God and that no person can ever come to heaven except through His shed blood. He was careful to avoid any mention of Mohammed or the Qur'an, focusing only on the fact that all are lost apart from Christ.

He spoke for fifteen minutes without any response from his Muslim audience, and he was growing discouraged when suddenly his wife, Hadhi, began to pray—loudly and fervently. She was praying in Amharic, not the tribal dialect; more startling still, she was rebuking the devil! Jirani was caught off guard by the unexpected interruption, and he urged her to stop.

"Hadhi!" he whispered. "You're going to anger them! And they have spears!"

But at that moment, Jirani noticed a dramatic change in those gathered underneath the tree: every person from eldest to youngest, male and female alike, raised their hands in an attitude of praise to God. He particularly noticed several women at the front of the group who were trembling violently. Amin, too, saw what was happening, and he whispered urgently into Hadhi's ear.

"Continue! Continue praying! Muslims need to see a miracle—and we are going to see something here today! So please: continue!"

"Lord Jesus," Hadhi cried in Amharic, "in your name I curse the wicked spirits of this place! I curse the spirit of rage! I curse the spirit of pride! I curse the spirits of envy and greed! Bind them, Lord—bind these evil spirits who hold these people in bondage. In the name of Jesus, I bind them!"

Jirani also began to pray, though he did so silently. "Lord, what do these people understand? They are accepting a prayer that they do not understand—and I don't understand! Oh Lord, within this time, and in this short prayer—please, Lord, let this day not be only for this day; let us come back again. Bring us back to this place."

Hadhi continued to call upon the Lord to bind demonic influences for several minutes, then abruptly she felt it was time to stop. The group under the tree recognized that the prayer had finished, and the men began to bow from the waist with their hands pressed together before them in a gesture of thanks. It almost seemed anticlimactic after the drama of a few moments before, yet Jirani and Amin politely returned the bow; then they began to talk quietly about what to do next. But at that moment, they were interrupted. A woman (Jirani recognized her as one of those who had been trembling during Hadhi's prayer) had grabbed the arm of the Muslim group's apparent leader and had rushed forward to confront them.

"She is asking the other guy," Jirani began to translate, "'are these people coming back again to our village?'" He then addressed the couple. "Why do you ask?"

The woman spoke rapidly for a moment, then the Muslim man addressed Jirani directly. "You see," said the Muslim leader, "she says that, while you were praying, she was shaking—she and her sister were trembling very hard. She said there was power in the prayer."

"What sort of power?" Jirani asked.

At this, the woman (whose name was Sabirah) could not restrain herself to custom and began to pour out her words. "While she was praying and I was shaking," she cried, Jirani translating as fast as he could, "something was leaving me. I could feel something *leaving* me! And now I feel much, much better! I feel free now! If you will just come back again and pray some more, there are so many things that can leave our area and our people. Oh please, say you'll come back!"

The man who was with her quelled her flow of words with a raised hand and significant look, and she grudgingly walked back to rejoin the others. Then the man turned back to Jirani.

"These women are saying, 'Will you come back?'"

"Yes," Jirani interrupted, "gladly! Yes! We would like to come back."

The man nodded without expression. "So," he said slowly, "you *want* to come back."

"Yes! Gladly!"

He continued to gaze at Jirani with a neutral countenance, giving away nothing of what he was thinking. "Well then . . . I think we have some questions first."

Jirani nodded assent, glancing at Amin in hopes of some clarification or guidance. The stranger, however, stepped close and tapped a forefinger against Jirani's chest.

"My name is Sad," he began (which actually means "good luck"), "and if you want to come back, we have three needs. First: we have no water in this region, and we need water." It was late August at this time, the height of the rainy season all over most of Africa, but this particular part of the country had been experiencing drought. "There is no water here, not anywhere in our region," Sad continued. "Our women must walk every day fifteen kilometers—each way—to fetch water. So: if you will bring us water . . . that's one."

"Second: we don't have a clinic in this area. Our children and our women are dying because they don't get any treatment. If you will bring us a clinic . . . that's two."

"And—question three: we don't have a school in this area either. If you bring us a school—if you bring us these three things—all three," he concluded, emphasizing each point with a jab of his finger, "then—then you can come back and continue."

Jirani had been interpreting the conversation, and at this point Amin leaned in. He looked the man in the eyes and said, "No."

Sad was startled. "No? But you said you *wanted* to come back. Why will you not bring us these things then?"

"There are two reasons," Amin explained while Jirani translated. "The first reason is that we don't have much money. We can't even bring *one* of these because we don't have money." Sad looked unconvinced, but Amin continued without waiting. "All the same, even if we had enough money to bring you all this, we would still not do it."

Sad began to look offended. "Why?" he demanded.

"Because we will not exchange water for the Truth of God. You must accept the teaching freely, no strings attached, no other demands or stipulations. But," he continued as Sad began to object, "but I will give you one guarantee: if we pray together, if you accept Jesus—if all of you accept Jesus—then Jesus can give us water, a clinic, and a school."

Sad snorted in disgust. "Jesus! How can *Jesus* bring us water if *you* cannot do it?"

"I said He can give us water, clinic, *and* school—not just water. This thing is very easy for God."

"Bah! Give me proof of this."

"No, I cannot give you proof. It is for you just to pray and wait. He will give us what—"

"So you will not give me proof?"

"No, I *cannot* give you proof! You must just pray and wait."

Sad leaned his face close to the two men. "Okay then," he said menacingly, once again jabbing his finger against Jirani's chest. "Okay then: you give me your telephone number. If *you* can't find proof, *I* will try to find proof! I will see for myself if this 'Jesus' can give us water, clinic, and a school." He straightened up. "And if He can," he added with a dismissive gesture, "well then, I will call you."

Jirani took a step backward at this. "Where are you going to get it?" he asked incredulously. "I have been a Christian for more than twenty years, but I could not give you evidence of this!" He noticed a smug look on Sad's face and hastened to add, "I do believe in prayer, my friend, and I believe in trusting God. But no one can give proof that prayer works! It is an issue of faith."

Sad smiled, then turned back toward his village. "You leave that to me," he said over his shoulder, stuffing Jirani's phone number into a pocket. "No proof, no preach. And if I find proof, I will call you."

The journey back to Yappa lacked the enthusiasm and anticipation of the trip out. Jirani was very disheartened by the strange events of the day. On one hand, he had seen the power of God moving in a dramatic way. But on the other hand, nothing seemed to have resulted from it. He brooded over the day, wondering whether he had made a mistake in thinking that the Lord had called him to this distant village. After all, the Lord had called him to minister at the little church in Yappa, the "Gospel Church for the World"—and this reminded him of his first conversation with Amin.

"So much for the 'world' part," he sighed.

Nevertheless, Jirani and Hadhi devoted time each day to intensive prayer. "Please, Lord," they prayed, "give these people evidence that you are able to give water, clinics, schools—whatever they need, you can provide it. Give them proof of this." They sensed that Sad, the village elder, was not interested. Yet others were, and there seemed to be some sort of spiritual warfare going on behind the scenes. Until God broke down the barriers, they could do nothing else but pray. They asked Him to open a door for them to return with the gospel, and they asked Him to teach them how to minister more effectively to a Muslim community.

And fifteen days later, He did. The young couple had just finished breakfast and were bowing in prayer together, when Jirani's cell phone buzzed.

"Hello?" said a strange voice. "Hello? Who are you?"

"I am Jirani. Who are *you*?"

"Oh . . . I am Sad. Pastor Jirani—I have proof! I have proof now that Jesus is able to give water. When can you come back and continue?"

So early the next morning, Jirani retraced his previous journey, this time by himself, and when he arrived outside the village, there stood the same fifty people under the same tree, standing patiently in the same attitude awaiting his arrival. The setting was the same, but his reception this time was markedly different. The people saw him coming from a long way off (he was on foot this time), and he suddenly heard the shrill ululation of the women's *ililta*, a high-pitched "la-la-la" cry used to welcome an honored guest or hero. Jirani was embarrassed by this treatment, but he had no choice except to keep walking. As he drew closer, the women ran toward him, still ululating, and the men followed behind wearing broad grins.

In a startling breach of custom, he found his arm gripped by Sabirah, one of the sisters who had stood shaking during his wife's prayer on the previous trip. "We are so glad you have come," she cried, pulling him forward toward the village. "Now you can pray for us some more, and more evil spirits will go away!" (Africans believe firmly in the reality of evil spirit beings. Their belief causes them to fear, which is the wrong response. Their fear causes them to attempt to placate the spirits, which is even worse. But they do not pretend that the spirit world is either a silly superstition or something to be investigated—and in this they are far wiser than many Americans.)

From that day on, Jirani visited that village twice a week, walking seven miles each way after riding the bus for hours. Sad would gather all the adults of the village under the old tree (and naturally all the children would follow), and Jirani would teach them stories from the Bible for the entire day, leaving himself only enough daylight to walk back to the bus. He taught them about creation and how God loved His creatures. He taught them how man had rebelled against God and how he had eaten from the tree of knowledge. He taught how God had prepared a way back to Himself, and how Abraham had believed God without any visible proof. He taught them about Jesus and His work of salvation—how He had come into the world to do what

Adam had failed to do, and that they could be born again into the family of God for which they had originally been created.

At the end of four months, fifteen people, including Sad and Sabirah, had accepted Christ and wanted to be baptized. The drought had not ended and there was still no water, so a group of twenty—including Amin and Hadhi and Jirani—all walked back to town to hold a baptism in a lake, while singing and dancing together the whole way. They deliberately took a circuitous route to the lake, passing through other villages along the way and singing praises to God while Hadhi played a "talking drum" (an hourglass-shaped drum with a head at each end that can be squeezed under the player's arm to change its pitch). Long before they reached town, the group of twenty had more than doubled; as they passed through town, it doubled again; and on that day more than one hundred men, women, and children watched as the new believers were baptized.

Each of those fifteen people led at least one family member to Christ over the following month, and another baptism took place—again with the very public demonstration of joy along the way. In the course of five months, most of that little village had come to believe in Isa al Masih, and the revival had spread into the surrounding villages and all the way back to town. Oh, there are so many more stories that we long to tell, if only there were time!

But there is one story that you'd probably like to hear: What proof did Sad find that convinced him that Jesus answers prayer?

LOVE YOUR NEIGHBOR

You have heard that it was said, "You shall love your
neighbor and hate your enemy." But I say to you,
love your enemies, bless those who curse you, do
good to those who hate you, and pray for those who
spitefully use you and persecute you, that you may
be sons of your Father in heaven; for He makes His
sun rise on the evil and on the good, and sends rain
on the just and on the unjust. For if you love those
who love you, what reward have you? Do not even
the tax collectors do the same? (Matthew 5:43–46)

Jesus clearly teaches us that we must love our neighbors, but He takes it one notch higher by instructing us
that we are to love our enemies as well! Loving those
who persecute us is very powerful and can be used of
God in very dynamic ways. The hardest places to reach
often yield the greatest fruit.

A year or so before the events of the last chapter, there was
an elderly man in his seventies named Ghulam living in a
village not far from where Sad lived. He had three wives and
nearly thirty sons and daughters, most of them grown with

families of their own; but his youngest son was just ten years old and still lived with him. This boy, whose name was Burhan, was not in his right mind. He would throw fits, convulsing on the ground and spewing profanity, interspersed with periods of great mental clarity—an almost disturbing clarity, for he had a penchant of pointing out people's faults and bad habits in the most embarrassing terms. Burhan also could not walk, although he had no physical disability; he simply could not stand on his feet. Instead, he moved about very fast by pulling himself along the ground with his hands in a spider-like motion that could be quite unnerving to those who didn't know him.

Ghulam didn't work. He preferred to amble into the nearby town (where the baptism took place in the last chapter) and join his shiftless friends chewing some khat and getting drunk. He was an intelligent man and was very skilled with woodworking—when he felt so inclined, which was not often. He would sometimes say that he could have made something of himself if it hadn't been for his bad habits, but his smarmy tone when he said it showed his friends that the problem was deeper than his addiction to khat.

The one thing that could sober Ghulam in a hurry was his son's illness, especially when a fit came on at an inconvenient moment. One day, he decided that he'd had enough of Burhan's outbursts, and he roughly picked the boy up and threw him over his shoulder. He walked hurriedly into town, dumped the ten-year-old in an alleyway, and went to join his friends in dissipation. "If he lives, let him live," he slurred to their glee. "And if not . . . well."

For many months after this, Burhan literally clawed his existence through that town, pulling his dead weight along the sidewalks, begging for handouts, snarling at those who ignored him, throwing lonely fits in dark alleys, scrambling to avoid feet and hooves and wheels, and feeding himself from piles of garbage. And even this dire existence grew more desperate as people became familiar with him—fearing the curses of his right mind, disgusted by the obscene rants that preceded the fits. Pedestrians crossed the street if he was begging, and vehicles would avoid him in the streets with only the barest margin. Burhan was aware, child though he was, that he would not likely see another birthday.

One Sunday morning (Palm Sunday, in fact), as Burhan was groveling at a corner, a cart drew up to the curb; a man climbed out. Burhan clawed quickly to the man's feet and begged for a coin, but the man drew up his robes in disgust. They were very white robes, thick and flowing and made of fine linen, and perhaps he didn't want them soiled. He was actually a high-ranking sheikh named Fakhir who had just arrived from Yappa, so it is also possible that his mind was occupied with loftier matters. Either way, he stepped roughly around Burhan and made his way hurriedly along the sidewalk, pedestrians and vehicles alike making way for his majestic passage.

Burhan, however, was following the sheikh's progress with a growling flow of profanity, draped over the curb like a pile of discarded rags. He was about to claw his way back to the corner when another pair of feet came down from the cart. He glanced upward with renewed hope, but these feet were not as promising—dusty and soiled from a long trip, with sandals rather than the previous tasseled loafers. Yet sandals were more than Burhan wore, so he quickly switched to his friendly begging face and held out his hand for a coin.

"I have no money for you," said a soft voice, "but I can give you something much better." Burhan considered some choice responses, but curiosity got the better of him. He looked up and waited without speaking. The man asked, "Would you like to walk?"

Not surprisingly, Burhan assumed that the man was mocking him, and his little face twisted in a huge rage. But before he could speak, the man said, "I am not making a joke. Jesus will heal you—if you let Him. But you must let Him." This Jesus, Burhan thought, must be some great doctor—maybe even a wealthy foreigner from the Western nations. He held his tongue.

"Do you want to be healed?" The stranger spoke in a tone that Burhan had never heard before, a tone of genuine love and compassion. The two remained gazing at one another for a few moments: man and boy, one upright and one crushed to the pavement, a frozen parable on the street corner. Then the boy spoke.

"Yes."

Instantly, the man stooped and gathered Burhan in his arms, grunting as he lifted (for he was a small man, not even as tall as Burhan's father), and he carefully positioned Burhan on the pillowed seat of the cart. Burhan looked around him and gasped. He had never sat in a chair before—never mind a taxi— and the seat beneath him was soft as goose down. But the view! He was gazing on the town from four feet in the air, not scanning it inches from his nose; more amazing still: people were gazing up to him—*up*! He was unaware that his face had been transformed with a boyish grin of delight.

The cart driver climbed up beside him and gave the reigns a shake. "Don't worry, son, Jesus will soon have you on your feet. Isn't that right, Ears?"

And so it was that Guma the "praying cartman" carried the boy to a missionary church nearby, toiling in with the welcome burden in his arms. This church, as it happened, was hosting a missions conference that week, and the hall was packed. Guma hesitated briefly at the door, searching faces for someone to help (they were all strangers to him, for he had carried the sheikh a long distance and was far from home), but nobody volunteered. Those from the area knew the boy and were fearful of his sharp tongue, while the many visitors (by far the majority that day) did not feel it their place to get involved. So Guma walked boldly through the crowd and made his way to the front, finally lowering Burhan gently to the dais—right next to the feet of the preacher.

The preacher stared in shock, not knowing what to say or do. Guma remained kneeling next to Burhan, who was trying to gather his uncooperative body into a ball. Then Guma raised his hands, looked toward heaven, and began to pray.

"Lord," he cried as the congregation grew hushed, "let this boy walk! Let his mind become right. Drive out the demons that bind him, and make him whole! In the name of Jesus, Lord, we ask for this!"

The preacher was completely at a loss; he was European, new to the work in Africa, and he was wondering whether this was the sort of thing he should expect in this culture. He turned toward an elderly deacon in the front row. "What is going on?" There was no time for an answer, for suddenly little Burhan lifted his head with a heartrending cry. He twisted and convulsed, his legs shooting in and out, hands grasping spasmodically.

"In the name of Jesus," cried Guma, "set this boy free!"

Burhan's body straightened, he spun sideways, gathered his legs together, and leaped upright like any normal boy playing a game. The congregation erupted in joyous shouts and laughter as Burhan did a little dance, bouncing into the air and kicking out his feet. Then he just as suddenly stopped, gazed at the congregation, burst into tears, and threw himself into Guma's open arms.

The preacher gripped his head in both hands. "What is this?" he shouted in astonishment. "I have never seen such a miracle!" But few people heard him or even noticed his histrionics, for the entire congregation had rushed forward to join Guma and Burhan in their embrace. As things gradually calmed down, however, the boy grew somewhat dazed and confused; he could not make sense of the whirlwind events of the morning, and he still didn't know who this Jesus was. (Guma, in standard fashion, had begun cheerfully telling Burhan about Jesus in the cart ride, but the child had been seized by a convulsion at the sound of His name.) Then the pastor regained some sense of order.

"Please," he said to Guma, thinking him the boy's father, "let this boy stay here in our compound." (The church had a walled courtyard with several buildings inside, offering the pretense of security in a town that was not overly friendly toward Christians.) "I will send him to school, and I will support him." Members of the congregation contacted Ghulam the next day and found him only too eager to foist his troublesome son onto the pastor's care—after gaining a few birr for his sorrow at the parting. Guma, meantime, had slipped away unnoticed, cheerfully talking to Ears and making notes in his prayer journal.

But Burhan wasn't the only one influenced that day by the praying cart driver. Sheikh Fakhir had traveled far and hard from Yappa with a single mission in mind: to confront the Christians in that town who were bringing Muslims to Christ. He and Guma had traveled long, dusty hours together in that little cart, and they had talked about Jesus the entire way.

Sheikh Fakhir knew his Qur'an from front to back, and he was a very crafty man. As soon as his driver had started "spouting Christianity," he had become smug in the expectation of turning him inside out intellectually. He had, of course, grossly underestimated his man, but he did not give up. He tried reciting the Qur'an, only to find that Guma knew it as well as he did. Then he switched to logic—"How could God, who is eternal, die on a cross?"—but he found himself becoming confused by the driver's counter-questions. He knew a little of the Bible, so he tried some tricks, saying that John the Baptist could not have baptized Jesus because Herod killed John, yet Herod himself died before Jesus was born![13]

He'd expected this last item to be a real stumper for Guma, but the exasperating driver remained unperturbed, merely smiling and asking, "What does that have to do with your salvation, my friend?" The sheikh eventually resorted to sheer bullying, being much bigger (and louder) than Guma. But nothing disturbed the little man's cheerful spirit. "I have faced death at the hands of a powerful gangster," he said at one point. "But shouting in my ear will not change your need for Jesus." It is little wonder, actually, that the sheikh was less than loving when confronted by a beggar after such a trip.

The fact is, however, that Guma was not the first man to confront this harried sheikh with the truth of the gospel. He had once been the right-hand man of Sheikh Jambres, prior to Jambres being introduced to the snake within the mosque, and he knew Amin quite well. This man, in fact, had been one of the major obstacles to Amin's ministry in Yappa, and the reason that Amin had brought the gospel to this distant region. Amin had been laboring here for months prior to recruiting Jirani; he had gotten to know many in the area, but he had seen little fruit. It seemed that the paths of the two men were destined to cross once again.

Two days after arriving, Sheikh Fakhir called all the faithful Muslims from the town and the outlying villages—a great many people—to gather at the town's mosque. It was a crowd that proved too large to fit inside. He stood in front of the mosque's bright turquoise doors and addressed the people.

"These Christians," he cried, "these Christians are cheating you! It is time to wake up! It is time to return to Allah! Some of your neighbors have been bought by these infidels. They have sold themselves into Christianity! Some of your own sons have done this! Your own children—some of *you* have sold yourselves to the infidels!

"And what did you get for it? Some wheat, some oil, some clothes? You have sold yourselves to the Christians for mere trinkets!" The missionary church had several ongoing ministries, one of which was to provide food, clothing, and medicines for the poor in the town and outlying villages. Ironically, it was not these ministries that were bringing Muslims to Christ, but the power of God working through ordinary men and women like Amin (and later, Sad and Sabirah); the food and clothing ministries, in fact, made no demand of recipients to accept Christ.

"So you have sold yourselves to the Christians—and this must stop!" The sheikh gazed thunderously on the crowd around him, and the people cowered under the charge of selling their souls, false though it was. Had the sheikh continued in this vein, the meeting might have ended differently. But he didn't.

"Yes!" he cried. "Yes! The Christians have cheated you!" He paused and smiled smugly. "We Muslims, though," he said in a softer voice, "we Muslims—we are *rich*! We are better than these Christians in finance—oh yes! And *we* can give you much more!" He grinned and nodded his head at the people as a rustling of whispers (and some laughter) spread through the crowd. "It is true, my people: we can give you more than these Christians—so why don't you come back to mosque?"

The sheikh raised his hands dramatically like a prophet delivering some oracle. "Now," he cried out. "Now! Right at this time today: we will buy you five oxen! Yes, we will kill them, right here today, and we will all eat together!" (These events took place during Easter week. The missionary church was holding its annual conference to bolster the many ministries in the region, and it culminated with a public banquet on Easter Sunday. Everyone was invited, and people would clog the streets around the church compound to enjoy the feast.)

"These Christians," the sheikh continued, "they feed you once a year—but we will do it every week! We can feed you every week, every Friday! So you must come back to Islam, because we can give to you better than they do."

Sheikh Fakhir could sense that his offer was making a stir amongst his audience, but he wasn't so sure it was the reaction that he'd anticipated—so he abruptly changed tactics.

"And listen—these Christians—they are teaching you false things! Jesus is not God, but they call on Him as if He *was* God!" The crowd was growing more restive, and he wanted to regain their attention—then he hit upon the magical words guaranteed to arrest any human audience. "Let me tell you a story," he said—and instantly the people stopped talking. "I will tell you a story, and after hearing it, I will not call you to come back. No, I won't need to: you will come back all by yourself. But just listen to this story."

"There was a man called Yahya—John the Baptist, the Christians call him. He was a prophet of Allah, and he did the work of Allah.[14] But did you know this? John the Baptist is just like today's Christians!"

Every face was turned toward him now, eyes and ears wide open—for the sheikh was going to tell them some new thing. "John the Baptist," said the sheikh, "his mind is just like today's Christians. You see, one day Jesus came to be baptized by John. He came walking." And here the speaker acted out his words. "He came walking one day to the river because He wanted to become baptized. So when Jesus reached the River Jordan, He called out, 'John, come and baptize me!'"

"Ah!" said Fakhir, dramatically lowering his voice. "Ah! But John, he said, 'No! I will never do such a thing, because you are God!' This is what John the Baptist said to Jesus: 'You are God,' he said, 'and I must be baptized by you! I will not baptize you,' he said, 'because you are God!'"

"But do you know what Jesus said? He said, 'No, I am a person like you! I am a human being just like you! So come now and baptize me.' This is what Jesus said. And John said, 'Oh! Oh,' he said, 'I thought you are God. But you are not; you are a person, just like me! Oh! If you are just like that, well then— come!' That is what John the Baptist said to Jesus!"

A few people clapped half-heartedly at this point, but any other effect that the story might have produced was undermined by the arrival at this moment of a half dozen armed police officers. These men pushed through the crowd, gently but authoritatively, and positioned themselves conspicuously near the mosque entrance, hands on hips and AK-47s slung over their shoulders. Another man had come forward in their wake, a government official in the region who was also the town's tribal chief. These men did not take control of the meeting, but they let the crowd know that they were present.

Sheikh Fakhir, initially frustrated at the interruption, became emboldened at the thought that he now had some official muscle behind him. He opened his mouth to continue, but a raspy voice from the crowd cut him short.

"Mr. Chairman," called the voice. "Chief, I have a question." The crowd turned to see an elderly man near the back raising his hand. It was no other than Ghulam, Burhan's father, who was better known in town as "Old Khat." Many smiled with the anticipation of whatever trouble the old reprobate was brewing. "I have a question," he called again.

"Okay," the chief responded, stepping forward in front of the sheikh. "You can ask."

"Chief," said Ghulam, "do you know Pastor Amin?"

"A man with a long black beard? Yes, I know him."

"Yes, that is the man I mean," Ghulam said. "Have you heard him preach his religion?" (Amin had often stood on street corners in this town, preaching the gospel to any who would listen.)

"Yes," answered the chief, visibly losing patience. "So?"

"So have you heard him, any time, preaching against Muslims? Have you?"

"No," the chief said tentatively.

"No. Have you ever heard him calling Muslims names on the street? Have you?"

"No, I have not. What is your point then?"

"My point is, Chief: What is this person doing?"—indicating the sheikh. "He is calling the name of this religion—calling on Christianity in this mosque—to make trouble!" Here was an unexpected turn of events. The town drunk was confronting a powerful sheikh, accusing him of stirring up trouble, and doing so boldly in the public square at that. There were no longer any smiles, any who anticipated some fun; things had suddenly taken a very serious turn, and the armed policemen shuffled uncomfortably. But Ghulam did not stop.

"This man creates conflict here; he wants anger between Muslims and Christians. I don't care," he said with a dismissive gesture, "Christian, Muslim—what do I care? But I see *him*—he has a political issue here, and he is wanting trouble. How do you stand and watch him, Chief?"

The chief's face had grown very grave. "Hmm . . . yes," he said, turning to the sheikh with a scowl. "Old Khat has a point for once. This will not do here!" He nodded significantly to one of the police officers, and the armed men moved forward in a tight body. This was a potentially explosive situation, and the tension in the crowd was palpable.

But Ghulam was still not finished. "You say you are going to kill us five oxen," he cried, moving forward through the crowd as he warmed to his topic. "Why didn't you do this two years ago? One year ago?"

"Because we've been forgotten," said a loud voice from the crowd. "Yes," echoed another. "We are forgotten people by our Muslim leaders!"

"It was a Christian person," Ghulam cried, now standing directly in front of the chief, "it was the pastor of the missionary church who remembered us! He and the Christians have given us food, clothes—even this sheikh admits it! So how does he stand here and say bad things about them?"

Things were deteriorating rapidly, and the chief determined to arrest the sheikh, as much to protect him as to defuse the situation. He said something to the officers, and they formed a circle around Fakhir. Then the unexpected happened again: Fakhir fell on his knees and grabbed the chief's leg.

"Please," he cried. "Please: let me go for today!" (Being imprisoned in Africa is no laughing matter—even if it's for your own safety—and the sheikh was terrified at the prospect.) "I will never come back again to this place! Don't put me in prison—I will leave immediately! Please, let me just go."

We might pity this man who had been so persistently frustrated by the hand of God over that week, yet God's purpose in such dealings is to lead a man to stop pushing *against* that hand—not to break his spirit. Fakhir chose to break rather than stop pushing, stubbornly refusing to bow before the Son of God even if it meant abandoning his followers. So the chief had the officers escort him out of town, and the people gradually dispersed without further incident.

And what was responsible for Ghulam's sudden and drastic change in behavior? Sad, the village elder from the last chapter, had at one time been one of Ghulam's drinking buddies and had joined in his self-indulgence whenever he was able to get into town. About ten days after the first visit of Jirani and Amin to Sad's village, he had gone to see Ghulam. His friend, however, had noticed that Sad was preoccupied and was not entering into their revelry with the usual gusto.

"So what is troubling you, Mosque-Builder?" (Sad had been very involved in earlier days with establishing and building mosques in the region.)

"We were visited by some 'hallelujahs' last week," he said. "They wanted to preach their religion to us." He glanced at his friend, expecting some snide response, but Ghulam did not mock.

"So?" Ghulam asked without turning his head. "What did you say to them?"

"Well . . . Okay, listen to this, then." Sad put aside his drink and turned earnestly to Ghulam. "I told them that they could come back if they brought us water, a clinic, and a school—to get rid of them, okay? But you know what the man said? He said, 'Jesus can give you these things if you pray'! What do you think of that?"

Ghulam gazed meditatively at the blank wall in front of them (for they were seated in a dank alley). Rather than answer, he opened another bottle and took a deep draught. Sad leaned back against the building, feeling inexplicably disappointed—though he could not have put that into words at the time. "Yes," he sighed, "that is what I thought too."

But his friend surprised him by setting down his bottle, standing slowly upright, and turning to face him. "Jesus is the One who healed my son. Made him walk, made his mind correct." For the next few minutes, Ghulam told Sad the entire story of his son's healing and salvation, omitting not the slightest detail—for it was a story that he had rehearsed and reflected on daily for the previous year, though he rarely spoke of it.

When he finished, Sad asked in a hushed voice, "So . . . it is true, then? You think this Jesus can bring us water?"

Ghulam held out his hands and cocked his head sideways. "Jesus is the man who healed my son, who made him walk!" he said, in an exasperated tone. "How difficult can it be for Him to bring you water?"

God sent water to that region soon after the events of the last chapter. He also later provided schools and clinics, but He used the hands of His people to build those things. He led Sad into contact with a missions group (one of Cityteam's partner organizations) that offered training on how to work most effectively in Muslim communities. Sad, Sabirah, and others learned how to look for a person of peace and how to use Bible stories to teach God's Word to people who cannot read. As the number of believers grew in the area, Sad and others led efforts in building several schools and clinics in order that the needs of their community could be met. Sad reasoned that learning to read could only help people to understand God's Word more readily, and he was able to use the skills he'd learned in his former efforts at building mosques.

Sadly, Ghumar died not long after these events, never taking the things he'd learned into his own heart. His lips acknowledged the power and authority of the Lord Jesus Christ, but he refused to yield his soul. Sheikh Fakhir took a similar route. He kept the letter of his promise by not returning to that town itself. But he did return to the outlying villages, bringing others with him; they created much hardship and persecution for the growing Christians, including Sad, Sabirah, and others whom we've met.

Several years later, Sad's entire village united to build a church for the growing body of believers—and they built it on land donated to them by the Muslims at the very mosque where Ghumar had confronted Sheikh Fakhir. The Lord used Sad, in fact, to establish a ministry in that area that has so far led more than twenty thousand Muslims to Christ. But these things did not come without persecution, as we're about to see.

11

SUFFERING

Beloved, do not think it strange concerning the fiery trial which is to try you, as though some strange thing happened to you; but rejoice to the extent that you partake of Christ's sufferings, that when His glory is revealed, you may also be glad with exceeding joy. If you are reproached for the name of Christ, blessed are you, for the Spirit of glory and of God rests upon you. . . . Yet if anyone suffers as a Christian, let him not be ashamed, but let him glorify God in this matter. (1 Peter 4:12–16)

If the world hates you, you know that it hated Me before it hated you. If you were of the world, the world would love its own. Yet because you are not of the world, but I chose you out of the world, therefore the world hates you. Remember the word that I said to you, "A servant is not greater than his master." If they persecuted Me, they will also persecute you. If they kept My word, they will keep yours also. (John 15:18–20)

Persecution is an instrument in releasing the power of the good news of Jesus. To turn around and love your enemy demonstrates that your life has been radically changed. Often the suffering or blood of the saints of Jesus lays the foundation for some extraordinary move of God.

Sabirah, the woman who had experienced release from demonic influence during Jirani's first visit to her village, was one of the village's first new disciples of Christ. Her husband, Maki, soon followed, for the couple had grown disillusioned with the ability of Islam to bring meaningful answers into their troubled lives. As they grew in wisdom and understanding of God's Word, they also grew in zeal to share that good news with others—particularly with people who were trapped within the Muslim culture as they had been. It wasn't long before they had begun a ministry of their own, traveling to towns and villages to share the gospel with anyone who showed an interest.

One day, the couple arrived in the large town where Burhan, the formerly handicapped boy, lived. It was a busy Saturday, and the main street was crowded with people buying, selling, chatting, and just passing through. In this part of Africa, boys and young men will set up an old chair, a discarded box, or even a rock—anything a person can sit on—and place it near the roadside, offering to shine the shoes of passersby for a coin or two. And on this day there were many of these little stands lining both sides of the street. The shoeshine process is very sociable, and people frequently stand about watching and chatting with one another, so Maki and Sabirah took advantage of this custom to talk with people—seeking someone who seemed interested in a casual conversation about eternal topics.

The couple had slowly made their way along the roadside when Maki noticed a very dark-skinned man having his shoes shined nearby. He was dressed as a sheikh, wearing the long flowing white robe with matching skull cap. These clothes would have drawn a viewer's eye by themselves, set dramatically against his black skin and beard, but this sheikh had added to the effect by hiking up his robes sufficiently to show off a pair of very expensive Italian shoes. He sat beaming a brilliant smile on all who passed by, frequently nodding and holding up a condescending hand of blessing. Rather than being surrounded by a few people gathered around to chat, this sheikh was accompanied by three young men, all dressed in Muslim robes and all scowling with threatening brows on any who dared to approach too close. Even the most naive observer would immediately recognize that this was a man of wealth and importance in that town, and all who went past were visibly awed in his presence.

Maki quietly took his wife's arm and nodded in the sheikh's direction. "Let us cross the street," he whispered. "We do not want to anger that man."

It happened, however, that the shoeshine boy glanced in their direction at that very moment, and Sabirah thought she detected a look of desperation in his eye. She hesitated a moment as her husband tugged on her arm, then planted her feet obstinately.

"No," she said firmly. "Let us not be afraid. That boy needs Jesus, too, so we must trust that Jesus will protect us." Without waiting for a response, she walked deliberately toward the young boy who was at the feet of the sheikh, her husband following with an expression of weary resignation (an expression that he wore frequently in his wife's company).

Sabirah squatted next to the shoeshine boy. "So how has business been today?" she asked pleasantly.

"So-so," he answered without looking up. "How has your harvest been?" This is a standard formula of small talk in such cultures, like discussing the weather with an American stranger. What made this conversation slightly unusual was that it was initiated by a woman, but the boy did not seem disconcerted. They chatted on this way for a minute or two, while the sheikh sat above them unaware of their existence.

"So where are you going?" the boy asked, following cultural protocol in such conversations.

"Oh," said Sabirah, "I have come here to see you!"

This comment caused the boy to sit up straight and turn to face her, his brush poised mid-stroke on the sheikh's shoes. "You came to see me?" he asked in a fearful tone. "Who is dead?" (In the countryside, where this boy lived, strangers only come for a visit when bringing bad news, such as a death in the family.)

But Sabirah broke into a smile. "Nobody is dead—in fact, that is why I came to talk with you." She leaned close to the boy's dirty face with a conspiratorial gleam in her eye. "I have a secret to tell you, but you must not repeat it!"

"Oh, no problem!" the boy exclaimed, his fear transforming into an excited grin.

"I don't have bad news," Sabirah continued. "I have good news. I want to tell you about Isa al Masih. This is glad news!"

By this time, Sabirah had the attention of more than just the shoeshine boy. The sheikh, whose name was Ali, had noticed that his beautiful shoes were not being served by the boy at his feet; he had bent a darkening brow upon the two conspirators whispering together. Maki was standing behind his wife, feeling fear growing in his breast. But his wife had not noticed. She began to tell the shoeshine boy a story about Isa, about His miraculous birth that had been foretold by prophets hundreds of years earlier. She told him that Isa was the Word of God, and told him that He had died but risen again from the grave. The boy was entranced, and a group of people had gathered to form a circle around them—at a respectful distance from Sheikh Ali—but no shoes were being shined.

"Where did you get these stories?" asked the boy (whose name was Tobias). "We don't have them in *our* Qur'an."

"Oh yes you do," Sabirah exclaimed. "These stories are in every Qur'an, but you don't get to read them because our sheikhs are not willing to tell us about them." A stunned silence surrounded her, but Sabirah didn't notice. "Me and you—our whole community—we have been in darkness for many years without knowing these truths. But we have come to you with the truth!"

The silence was suddenly broken with a bellow from above. "This is a disgrace!" a man's voice roared. "This woman is disrespecting me!" Sabirah looked up to find Sheikh Ali towering above her, his face contorted with rage.

Maki had been frozen in place when he saw the man rise, but now he grabbed his wife's arm and pulled her to her feet. The crowd around them had moved back a pace when the sheikh rose, but the couple was still hemmed in and unable to walk away.

"Do you see me, woman?" Sheikh Ali cried in commanding tones. "Do you see my long beard? Do you see my clothes? Do you not know that I am a very religious man?" Sabirah, frightened herself now, stood looking at the ground and saying nothing. "How dare you do this in the street, not three meters away from me!"

Sheikh Ali majestically snatched his robes about him, avoiding defilement from a woman preaching Christianity to a shoeshine boy, and turned to face the young men behind him. "Go! Buy pepper. This woman will weep for her sins!"

Without further instruction, the three men pushed their way through the crowd and disappeared. Maki, still gripping his wife's arm, hustled her away in hopes of avoiding any further confrontation. The street was long, and after a hundred yards of hasty walking, Sabirah felt it was safe to try talking with a friendly shopkeeper. Maki, content to follow his wife's lead, allowed his vigilance to lag. Consequently, he did not see the three angry men approaching until it was too late.

The men stepped up behind the couple as one of them viciously grabbed Sabirah's right arm and spun her about. Each had a handful of cayenne pepper that they threw into the couple's faces as if on cue, using a slightly upward angle in hopes of insinuating the powder into nostrils and under eyelids. The skill and coordination of the attack, in fact, suggested that they had done it before. Instantly, both Maki and Sabirah cried out in pain, frantically brushing their faces in a vain attempt to remove the pepper. Mucus, tears, and saliva flowed from their chins as the powder burned its way inside like tear gas; both rolled helplessly to the ground. "Let Isa heal your eyes," snarled the man who had grabbed Sabirah's arm. Then all three melted into the crowd once more.

Chaos ensued. A large crowd gathered to look at the couple, writhing and weeping on the ground, and all traffic came to a standstill. Horns blared, drivers cursed, donkeys brayed, people shouted and pointed—but nobody dared to help the Christians. In short order, several policemen arrived to break up the crowd and get traffic moving again—which they accomplished with universal police logic by arresting the injured victims. The couple was dragged off the street, tossed into a VW minibus, and carted away to the town jail.

Meanwhile, Sheikh Ali had made his way in full dignity back to his office, where he sat reading his Qur'an. An hour or so later, he found a police officer at his door with a warrant for his arrest.

"What is your name, Officer?" he demanded, drawing himself to his full height and glaring down on the hapless policeman.

"Mohammed," the officer answered sheepishly.

"Mohammed! You are a good Muslim, no?" The policeman nodded humbly, clearly uncomfortable with his duty. "Well, Mohammed, the reason I had my boys deal with that woman was because she was telling people about Jesus—right in front of myself! She was disrespecting me. You are not disrespecting me, are you?" The sheikh leaned a glaring face close to the officer's.

"No!" the officer declared, pushing out his chest. "You were right, father. This punishment was not enough for her!" And with that, the policeman turned on his heel and left. A few hours later, however, two more officers arrived. This time they would not be dissuaded. Sheikh Ali had to return with them to the police station to sort out what had happened.

The sheikh arrived at the little compound, escorted by one of the officers. As he entered the main building, an elderly woman approached the officer, reaching out to shake his hand. "Not now, Miss Hannah," the officer said, pushing past her, "this is not a good time." Miss Hannah smiled and returned to her chair in the corner, while Sheikh Ali adjusted his eyes to the dim interior light. The room was crowded with police officers and citizens, for there had been several other arrests in the disturbance and the harried desk sergeant was unable to process them all. As Ali's eyes grew accustomed, however, he spotted the young couple standing near the sergeant's desk. He drew himself up grandly, head thrown back and chest out, and pointed dramatically in Sabirah's direction.

"That woman!" he cried in a voice that would have filled the largest mosque. "That woman disrespected me—in public! She sat at my very feet, teaching Christianity to a shoeshine boy. A shoeshine boy!"

Silence fell inside the police station. Even the sergeant at his desk turned to gaze upon the accused woman. Sabirah stood against the far wall, her face streaked with moisture and her eyes swollen shut. If she had forced herself, she might have been able to squint through the burning lids to see her accuser—but she had no need. Turning her face in the direction of his voice, she raised a hand and pointed right back.

"Please," she said to no one in particular, "please, I don't want that man to be put in prison. Please let him go."

If anyone in that crowded room had not been paying attention before, he was now. The desk sergeant sat staring at her over the rim of his glasses with an angry scowl (gestures that were wasted on Sabirah). "It has cost us much trouble to bring this man here," he growled. "Do you know who he is? He is a very important sheikh in this town!"

"I don't need to know who he is," Sabirah answered, wiping moisture from her face. "Jesus knows who he is, and He will take care of this. Please: let him go."

The desk sergeant debated quietly with the arresting officers for several minutes, then he raised a stony face to the sheikh. "You may go," he said with a tight-clenched jaw. Sheikh Ali stood a moment dumbfounded. He had been expecting much haggling and aggravation from the police. He had come prepared to barter, threaten, pull rank, and even bribe if necessary to obtain his release. This sudden change of fortunes, ironically, annoyed him; for in some sense he now felt that he was indebted to the very woman who had so grievously insulted his dignity a few hours earlier. He turned in her direction.

"Let this be a lesson to you," he blustered, not able to think of anything more haughty on the spur of the moment. "Do not preach your Christianity in the streets of *my* town ever again!"

Sabirah could not see him across the room, but she spoke without lifting her head. "May Jesus meet you on the way," she said.

Sheikh Ali's jaw dropped in astonishment. "What?!" he cried.

"May the Lord meet you on your way," Sabirah repeated.

"Bah!" spat the sheikh. "This punishment is not enough for you! I will get you another time!" He spun around in a rage and stormed out of the police station.

That night, the sheikh slept fitfully. The woman's strange words kept coming into his head: "May Jesus meet you . . . may Jesus meet you." The next day, and for many months to come, Sheikh Ali began to inquire discreetly about this strange woman and her Jesus. He was told, "She follows Jesus"—hardly a revelation—so he began to seek information on Jesus within the Qur'an. What motivated his study was his own long-standing dissatisfaction with the doctrines and practices of Islam (although he kept such doubts a deep secret, not wanting to imperil his standing in the town), coupled with a growing respect for Sabirah's patience and forgiveness. "If those who follow Jesus have such huge patience . . . ," his conscience kept saying, ". . . well, I *need* that patience!" And so began a time of deep study and research, through the Qur'an as well as the extended writings of Islam, in search of information concerning this Isa al Masih, Jesus the Messiah.[15]

One night, Ali had a dream. He saw a sheikh, a very great man—great in every way, for he was of tremendous size, looming over a crowd of people gathered by his knees, glaring at them in a dreadful wrath. The people trembled in his presence. Many bowed themselves to the ground; others beat their breasts in anguish, as many, many more people came from every direction to join the throng. Ali saw that the people were begging for forgiveness from the great sheikh—but he steadfastly refused. Hundreds, thousands, countless masses of grieving people flocked before him—each begging to be forgiven of his or her crimes. But the giant was adamant. There could be no forgiveness, he said, because there was no forgiveness to be had. Beg and tremble and cry out as they liked, the mourners would find nothing but wrath and vengeance.

Ali began to tremble himself, and sweat poured from his body. "This sheikh," he said to himself, "he is in charge of everything! I cannot hope to escape him because he has complete authority." And he crumpled to his knees in despair and began to weep.

But then he heard a loud voice, like an announcement coming over some invisible loudspeaker. "Vacancies! We have vacancies for soldiers! There is still room—sign up and become a soldier!"

"Oh, why not?" Ali said. "What have I got to lose now?"

So in his dream, Ali signed up to become a soldier and then found himself walking through a military camp. Many tents were standing all around him, neat and white in the sun, orderly rows lined up in every direction as far as his eye could see. Many other soldiers were bustling to and fro, but what struck Ali was the difference between these people and the ones who trembled before the huge sheikh: these soldiers were smiling! They were rugged and tough looking, like well-disciplined fighters. They appeared proud to wear their uniforms, pleased to be serving in this huge military camp.

Then Ali noticed a large cache of weapons nearby. He walked over and examined them, and he was amazed to find nearly every kind of firearm and weapon—automatic rifles, shotguns, high-caliber pistols, even rocket-propelled grenade launchers! Every weapon, wielded by modern soldiers and "freedom-fighters" alike, was lying in a pile as though they had been carelessly discarded. He hefted an AK-47, a rifle that he was familiar with, and found that it was working perfectly, well-oiled and clean and ready for action.

"With these weapons," he thought, "I could kill my enemies. Why—I could even kill that sheikh!" Yet here the weapons lay in a heap, as though they were worthless.

Then the dream shifted again, and Ali found himself standing atop a lofty mountain. He was no longer in a military camp, surrounded by white tents; now he was in a quiet neighborhood surrounded by peaceful houses, once again stretching as far as his eye could see reaching all the way down the mountain. But it was very quiet here—too quiet. He realized that there were no people anywhere. Then he noticed another odd thing: the houses were normal African dwellings, but they had no doors. Windows, but no doors! "How do these people come home with no doors to get inside?" Ali wondered. "Or . . . what if they are *already* inside! Maybe the people who live here are trapped inside their own homes!" A sense of horror came over him at this thought, a revulsion as though the people had been buried alive.

Then he heard a rustle and turned to face the mountaintop. Here came another huge man—bigger than the giant sheikh, so much bigger and greater that Ali was filled with fear. But this man looked different; he was dressed in white, and he had military insignia on his chest and shoulders. "This is the Great General," Ali thought, "coming to make me a real soldier at last." Then he noticed a very strange thing: as the General walked toward him, moving swiftly down the mountainside street, the doors of the houses, invisible to him before, were now suddenly bursting open. Each time he moved past a house, its front door would burst open with a resounding bang. And now the streets were filling with people, pouring forth from those houses and following silently behind the General.

And then Ali found himself standing before the great man. The General touched his shoulder. "Ali," he said in a strong voice, "did you get all the guns?"

"Yes, General," he replied, "I got all the guns." Then he looked down and realized with a shock of dismay that his hands were empty. "Oh, what kind of soldier am I?" he cried inwardly. "The General will be angry—what kind of soldier has no weapon?"

But then he noticed that the General was handing him something. "This is your weapon," he said. Ali found himself holding a small, compact weapon of a type he had never seen before. He knew right away that it did many things—much more than simply shoot bullets or grenades. "I don't know what it looked like," he said later, "but I know what it felt like: pure power—raw energy!" But he had no time to experiment with it, for the General was speaking again.

"You thought you could kill the sheikh with a gun," he said, "but you were wrong. You cannot kill the sheikh—only I can do that. In fact, I have already defeated him—he just doesn't know it yet. This weapon is far more powerful than a gun. It does not take life—it gives it! It can belong to you; it will be yours—if you will follow me."

In the weeks that followed this dream, Ali spent countless hours, whole days, poring through the Qur'an in search of understanding of Jesus. He found this passage, among many others:

> And remember when Allah said: O Jesus! Lo! I am gathering thee and causing thee to ascend unto Me, and am cleansing thee of those who disbelieve and am setting those who follow thee above those who disbelieve until the Day of Resurrection. Then unto Me ye will all return, and I shall judge between you as to that wherein ye used to differ. As for those who disbelieve I shall chastise them with a heavy chastisement in the world and the Hereafter; and they will have no helpers.[16]

Elsewhere he found:

> O mankind! Now hath a proof from your Lord come unto you, and We have sent down unto you a clear light; As for those who believe in Allah, and hold fast unto Him, them He will cause to enter into His mercy and grace, and will guide them unto Him by a straight road.[17]

Ali's heart filled with joy. "At last," he thought, "I have found the way to heaven." He knew that it had been this Jesus who had appeared to him in his dream, and he determined that he would follow Him and obey His commands like a good soldier to his general. The problem was, however, that he did not know how.

He gradually became aware that he was not alone in this conundrum. One day, he stumbled upon a group of nine men, all Muslim sheikhs like him, who were secretly meeting together for study and discussion. They, too, had discovered a prophet named Isa in the pages of the Qur'an, and they wanted to know more. So Ali joined them, and together they began to comb carefully through every page of the Qur'an, dividing amongst themselves the more extended Islamic writings contained in the Hadith and elsewhere—all the time searching for any information concerning the prophet called Isa. And the more they studied together, the more convinced they became that they needed to obey Isa if they were to find peace with God.

But at this point, a division developed within the group of sheikhs. Five of the men said, "We are discovering some very important things—things that will force us to go against our traditional Muslim teachings if we obey them. We must not do that! If we continue, we will be destroyed; we will be killed!"

The other five, including Ali, argued against this fear. "Why should we be afraid of people?" they said. "It is God that we should fear. If people kill us, then Isa will resurrect us! We must go out and learn more about Isa from those who follow Him."

"But the followers of Isa don't exist anymore," cried the fearful men. (Islam teaches that the true writings of Christ have been corrupted and no longer exist, that the Bible used by Christians is not the true Word of God, and that those who claim to follow Jesus do not have any source of knowledge about Him—they are merely compromising with the world.)

"Well, if that is so," Ali said boldly, turning from man to man, "if there are no true followers of Isa—well, why don't *we* become the ones? And if we die, Isa will resurrect us! So let's go out and look for this truth."

Half the group of men did in fact go out shortly after this debate, but they were not seeking Jesus; they were dissociating themselves from Ali and the other "zealots" who insisted upon continuing the search for truth. Those who remained determined together that they would go forth and look for the true followers of Isa, if in fact any such people still existed.

This, however, proved to be a huge undertaking. The sheikhs had never paid much attention to the Christians in their region previously, but now they discovered a strange phenomenon: denominations. Some of the five men had gone to visit Orthodox or Catholic churches, and Ali's share had fallen to whatever was left over—and he was overwhelmed with what he found. He is quick to add today that a Christian is not defined by any denominational label, for no church can offer salvation—it is the gift of God through Christ alone—but in the year or more that he spent in search of the true followers of Isa, he found his hope of answers dwindling away.

Sifting through the denominational issues was daunting enough, but Ali encountered an even more difficult barrier in his search for the truth: people. Right from the beginning, he felt that he was different from the people in his region who called themselves Christians. Part of this was nobody's fault, for Ali was a member of a tribe that was not well represented in the area, and he found no tribal affiliation at the churches he visited. Another issue was a language barrier, since all the services were conducted in Amharic—as were the Bibles—and Ali did not have a strong mastery of that language. Beyond these issues loomed the basic fact that the Christians were all at least second-generation, which meant that there were no Christ followers who had formerly been Muslims.

But there was another human barrier Ali had to surmount; the Christians at those churches were just as uncomfortable with him as he was with them. This region had a history of violent outbursts against Christians, and Ali still looked outwardly like a Muslim sheikh—a very large, intimidating Muslim sheikh. The deacons in those churches fulfilled a secondary duty as watchmen—*gatekeepers* is the word that Ali uses—who kept a wary eye open during all meetings to avoid any unexpected attacks, and they invariably became agitated whenever he showed up on a Sunday morning.

On one such occasion, Ali entered a large home where Christians had gathered for worship. (Remember that many African Christian churches meet in homes, not in large buildings with a steeple on top.) He had made a concerted effort on this Sunday to wear neutral clothing in hopes of being less off-putting to those he met, but as he stooped to enter the building, his eyes were met by one of the deacons. The Christian's eyes did an involuntary sweep of Ali, quickly scanning from head to toe, taking in the large turban atop his head, the bristling black beard that hung down nearly to his waist—"I think he was just a little bit terrified," Ali laughingly explains today.

"What do you want?" asked the timorous deacon.

"I want to talk to your leader." The deacon made a tentative gesture toward another room, so Ali entered, threaded his way into the group of people, then seated himself with them on the floor. And one by one, the people around him stood up and left. As they jostled one another to climb past Ali, many of the Christians muttered "in the name of Jesus, in the name of Jesus," and a few crossed themselves. The group grew smaller as Ali waited to speak with the pastor—but the pastor did not materialize, and the worship did not begin.

"I came for a reason," Ali said to anyone who would listen. "I came because I want to understand Isa al Masih." But no one would respond; no one dared to engage him in conversation. "Why do you keep leaving?" he asked one man who had been trying to slip past him unnoticed. "What is wrong? Is it my clothes? Do my clothes carry the devil?" But his clothes were not the issue; the Christians were fleeing Ali's presence simply because they were afraid of *him*.

Ali felt sad and lonely, but as he left the meeting his reaction grew into anger. He returned home determined to abandon the quest; if Christians don't want *me*, he fumed, why should *I* want *them*? Yet this did not bring any satisfaction, for there was a force at work inside his soul that he did not understand—some nagging sense that he needed to know this Isa if he was to find the peace and answers he so desperately sought. And to learn more about Isa, he felt compelled to find the true followers of Isa—if any such still existed—so he steeled himself to face the humiliation, and returned to that home-church the following Sunday.

And on this occasion, the pastor also steeled himself with courage when he saw the frightening man entering his door once again. Others in the congregation unintentionally made room for Ali to sit down, their eyes wide as they scooted in all directions, and the pastor came over and sat down in the resulting space.

"Okay," he said, crossing his legs in businesslike fashion, "what do you want?"

"I don't want to be alone," Ali burst out, surprised by the vehemence of his own answer. "I want to believe in Isa—I want to be a part of *you*!"

The pastor was understandably taken aback. "So . . . you are going to . . . accept the Lord?" He squinted his brows together as though he were trying to understand some difficult concept.

"I am not sure what you mean 'accept the Lord,'" Ali responded, furrowing his own brows. "I want to follow Jesus—that is what I do know."

The pastor looked a trifle relieved. "Oh, I see," he said. "Let me give you some books!"

"No!" Ali held up a vehement hand. "I have enough books! I know who Jesus is: He is 'the light' from heaven, and He is 'the way' from God. Just tell me what I need to do to obey Him."

So the pastor called together the elders and some of the older men of the church, and they all knelt in a circle around Ali and began to pray. "They spent an hour chasing demons from me," Ali now says with a chuckle, "somebody holding my shoes, someone holding on to my clothes, somebody holding my head—everybody got a part of me, and started chasing demons from my life."

This would have been an outrageous affront—or worse—to most Muslims, but Ali understood that those people were sincerely trying to help him find the truth of Jesus, so he humbly submitted. After a time, however, the prayers and enthusiasm waned, and gradually silence returned to the home.

"You have not fainted or shouted," said the pastor after a moment. (They had expected Ali to show outward signs of being delivered from demons, and were disappointed by the result.) "This is an unbelief in you."

The humans involved in this interaction were clumsy and fallible, but they were not alone: the Holy Spirit was there, too, and somehow Ali found himself desiring all the more to know

Jesus and to serve Him. "Okay," he said, trying a different tack. "I want to read the Bible now. Help me do that."

The Christians gave him a Gideon New Testament, and Ali left feeling that he'd made some progress—but not enough. He did not feel comfortable with the New Testament because he knew that it was incomplete, it was not the whole Bible. So the next day, he went into a larger city where there was a Christian bookstore, anticipating that he could get a complete Bible there. It was in a section of the city that afforded more luxurious stores, sporting large showcase windows such as are common in the West. Inside one window was a display of Bibles, and Ali felt confident that he'd come to the right place. Unfortunately, he was still wearing his turban and sporting his aggressive beard.

"I'd like to buy a Bible," he told the man behind the counter.

"We don't have any," was the reply—without a pause or so much as a blink.

Ali was dumbfounded. "But you have them—*there!*" He pointed emphatically toward the window behind him. Now the clerk began to shuffle his feet, obviously becoming nervous.

"Oh . . . those," he mumbled. "Yes, well . . . they are two hundred birr." The price tags in the window stated twenty birr. Ali considered giving the man a genuine reason to be nervous, but after a moment he unknowingly imitated Jesus.

"Fine," he said with a smile. "I will pay your two hundred birr."

Treatment like this in a Western store would have been followed by lawsuits and front-page news articles—indeed, Ali himself would never have stood for it just a few months earlier—but this day he simply walked back home carrying his large Bible with a gold cross embossed on the cover. (He immediately removed the cross when he got home, feeling that it was a manmade embellishment to God's holy Word.) That night, he had another dream, in which he saw himself standing still while hundreds of worms came wriggling out of his body. "I was being cleaned," he explains today.

The next day, he placed the Bible in a heavy leather case that had previously held his Qur'an, grabbed his supply of khat, and sat himself down underneath a tree to read. Whenever someone walked past, he would put on his best sheikh-like mien and look as though he was studying the Qur'an. (The khat, as it happened, was more than a mere prop in his charade. He had been a heavy user of the drug, as well as tobacco products, for many years. But as time passed in his daily routine of Bible study, Ali found his cravings disappearing.) Over the course of time, things became much more clear. Ali was at last on his way to understanding what it means to love and obey Jesus the Messiah, and even the followers of Christ didn't stand in the way.

Now, you'll remember that Ali had begun his quest for the true Christ followers along with four other men, the remainder of the original ten sheikhs who were seeking Jesus. While Ali's story was unfolding, God had been just as busy in the lives of the others. They, too, were continuing to meet together regularly, and around this time they all agreed to share what they were learning with other Muslim sheikhs. Each man chose one sheikh whom he knew personally and set out to teach him about Isa al Masih—the Jesus of the Bible.

"Nobody told us what to do," Ali says today. "Nobody was studying with us. We just had a new boldness, a new understanding, and we wanted to share it with others."

And share it they did. Within a short time, each of the five men had brought another Muslim sheikh into the Bible study, returning the group to its original ten. Now they just needed a safe place to meet. Ali approached the elders at the home church once again.

"I have ten people—ten *sheikhs*—and we want to study the Bible. Can you give me a room to teach them in?"

The elders all excused themselves into the next room, where a heated debate took place. One said, "He's lying! He doesn't really have anybody. Who ever heard of ten sheikhs wanting to study the Bible?!" Another said, "Okay, he might have *some*—I mean, *he's* a sheikh, so maybe he has another friend or two. But if we give them a room, persecution will come upon us!"

But after much struggle and discussion (and, one hopes, prayer), the elders offered the sheikhs one room at the back of the building for their Bible studies. So Ali and his friends began that very week, all ten of them, to study the Bible together in that little back room. For the safety of the Christians who lived and met there, they were careful to remove any clothing or outward indications that would identify them as sheikhs—lest they inadvertently bring persecution upon the other Christ followers. Ali also purchased Bibles for each of the sheikhs—ones that were translated into their tribal dialect—and they also brought their Qur'ans. Ali was showing the men the Qur'an's teachings about Isa then moving them into the Bible to find the full truth of Jesus.

But this did not sit well with the church elders. "What are you doing?" they asked. "We thought you wanted to study the Bible."

"We do study the Bible," Ali patiently answered. "But we also want to know how we can share Jesus with other Muslims—and this means, as former sheikhs, that we must also know how to show people that Jesus is in the Qur'an."

"This is not our traditional way," the elders answered. "Don't bring them here again."

This was a crushing blow, and the ten men shuffled back out of the church with bowed heads. One of the elders, however, had been their advocate from the beginning. He rushed after them.

"I have a small farm outside of the city," he said. "You can come to my home—it is not big enough inside, but you can use my backyard. It isn't much, but it's all I can offer you."

This small gesture of love filled the men with joy, and they grabbed the elder's hand and nearly carried him all the way to his home. Another believer from the church lived near that elder, and he immediately offered the men full use of his house when they needed it. This sudden embrace from the followers of Jesus was all the encouragement those men needed, and within a few weeks their Bible study had grown to forty—all Muslim sheikhs. (By this time, Ali and his original four friends had become committed followers of Jesus Christ, and described themselves as former sheikhs. Some of the others in this large group, however, had not yet accepted Christ as their Savior.)

For the next year Ali continued to teach these men from the Scriptures, and within that time all forty had accepted Christ. The church elders also spent that year teaching Ali personally about the doctrines of baptism. "They had to teach me for a full year before I could be baptized," Ali now laughs, "to make sure I was properly saved." But whatever Ali learned from the elders, he faithfully took back to his group and taught them as well.

The baptism itself was a large hurdle for the former sheikhs to overcome. "If Jesus got baptized for us," they asked, "why do we need to be baptized?" They studied the Gospels together, and discovered that Jesus was baptized out of obedience to the

Father and that He then commanded His disciples to do the same. "Ah," said the former sheikhs, "now we see. Jesus commands us, so we must obey."

More than half the men insisted upon being baptized as soon as possible—but the local Christian churches were afraid. An open baptism of former Muslim sheikhs could only end in violence, they feared, and there were few willing to take that risk. Around that time, however, Dawit came to the city to conduct a funeral. After talking with some of the local Christians, he learned of Ali and his friends, and immediately offered his assistance with the baptism. He had originally intended to conduct the funeral and head home the same day, but he agreed to stay over another day—and what a glorious day that proved to be! In a secret place off in the bush, twenty-six former Muslim sheikhs openly declared their new birth in Christ by being baptized in a small brook.

Over the course of time, God has used Ali and his friends to disciple more than fifty former Muslim sheikhs, and they have seen more than five thousand households embrace God's gift of eternal life through Jesus Christ. Most of these Christ followers live in areas where Muslim persecution can be very intense, so we cannot be too specific, but many of the former sheikhs have become elders in their villages because they are highly respected—even by those who are still in the grip of Islam. Many of these regions formerly suffered under extreme poverty, but God has poured out His blessings upon both the people and the land. Abundant crops have resulted in villages doing more than merely feeding their families, which in the past was the best they could hope for; now, the villagers have enough left over to open trade with other regions, and the Lord is using that to spread the gospel as well.

The baptism went late into the afternoon, so Dawit agreed to spend one more night in the village and to head home the next morning, preferring to make the long trip in daylight since his motorcycle had been running unreliably lately. But those plans, too, were going to change.

12

RESURRECTION

And as you go, preach, saying, 'The kingdom
of heaven is at hand.' Heal the sick, cleanse the
lepers, raise the dead, cast out demons. Freely
you have received, freely give. (Matthew 10:7–8)

Jesus gave an instructional message to His disciples on
how to serve people and care for their needs. And in
the middle of a sentence, He unloaded a bombshell:
raise the dead! In a conflict of cultures, Jesus declared
war in a direct encounter with the forces of evil holding
captive men's souls. Death is so powerful in all cultures;
each culture has developed a method of dealing with its
finality, but none of them expect someone who is dead
to come back to life! When someone does, it is immediately known that this God is the all-powerful One!

A round eleven o'clock on the night of the baptism, Dawit's cell
phone rang just as he was getting into bed, and an agitated
woman began speaking before he even said hello. Her name was
Tawbah, and she was the sister of Quadir, the gangster whom
Guma the cart driver confronted in a previous chapter. Tawbah
had returned to her village after that encounter with dramatic

stories of the power of a man named Jesus, and her family had listened enthralled as she told of the things that had happened to her brother and father. Guma had also given her a Bible, and her husband, Ubaid, had begun to read it to her and their children. One evening, they read Jesus' words: "He who has My commandments and keeps them, it is he who loves Me. And he who loves Me will be loved by My Father, and I will love him and manifest Myself to him" (John 14:21). Tawbah and Ubaid realized that, if they were to gain peace with God, they needed first to obey the teachings of Jesus—and in that hour they became committed followers of Christ.

On the night she phoned Dawit, however, Tawbah's heart was filled with anguish. "Pastor Dawit," she said over the phone, "my friend Guma gave me your number. He said I should call you right away. My daughter is very sick. They say she is dying. Please! We need your help. Can you come?"

Dawit was able to piece together the basic story from the distraught mother. Her daughter, twelve-year-old Hayat, had suddenly taken ill the day before, and by the early morning her condition had grown alarming. Tawbah had taken her to a nearby clinic that evening, and the doctor had been very grave. "Just take her home and make her comfortable," he said, "because she is dying. There is nothing we can do." In desperation, the mother had been driven to her network of Christian friends, while her husband had been driven to his knees. After many hours in prayer and phone calls, Tawbah had gotten hold of Dawit.

The family lived about ten kilometers away from where Dawit was staying that night, and he threw his clothes on and took a hasty departure from his host. The night air was bitter cold, but he knew the trip should take less than half an hour on his motorcycle, and he borrowed a jacket to keep warm. Before the night was over, however, Dawit would wish he'd added mittens and a scarf to his wardrobe because the drive was destined to be far longer than anticipated.

His motorcycle had been giving him some problems recently, sputtering unpredictably and sometimes being hard to start, but tonight it outdid itself. He climbed astride it, settled into his helmet, and pressed the ignition button. The starter cranked and cranked, but the engine refused to catch. He switched off the headlamp and tried again, hoping to get more juice into the equation, but still the engine would not turn over. He let it rest a moment, then pressed the starter. There was a loud *pop*, and the starter motor took on a mind of its own, cranking and cranking even after Dawit released the button. The engine sputtered but didn't catch, while the starter kept turning over, and then there was another pop followed by a sizzle, and everything went dead. Lifting the seat, Dawit discovered that something had short-circuited, actually melting one of the battery terminals and disconnecting the power.

With trembling hands, he managed to jury-rig the battery connections, then began jumping on the kick-starter. "Lord," he prayed feverishly, "make this thing start. Please!" The bike instantly coughed to life, and Dawit breathed his thanks to God as he sputtered into the darkness, his headlamp barely illuminating his way.

But this was just the beginning of a long night of frustration. He was navigating a narrow dirt path when a stick ripped the chain from its sprockets, and Dawit spent more than half an hour bloodying his knuckles to get it back on. He took a wrong turn at a fork in the road because he didn't have enough light to see clearly. The bike developed a new quirk, stalling inexplicably even as he roared along, so that Dawit had to keep popping the clutch at thirty miles an hour to restart it. He ran out of gas, even though the tank had been more than half full when he'd started, and he wasted more precious time knocking on doors to find someone who would sell him fuel. Even the elements seemed pitted against him, for he was tormented by a strong headwind that blistered his face and hands, a wind that seemed to blow straight at him no matter which way he was heading. The sick child was only ten kilometers away, but she might as well have been across the African continent, and Dawit was at wit's end to understand what was happening.

Then he recognized that he was in the middle of a spiritual battle, and he began to pray in earnest. "Lord," he cried out as he lurched along the road, "this child is going to die! Please go before me, Lord. Prepare the way. Save this child!" At one point, he sheepishly realized that he was praying at the top of his lungs. He lowered the helmet's face shield, "So people wouldn't think I'm crazy," he said later. But by this time, there wasn't a soul on the road to hear him. "And Lord," he cried, "bind Satan. In the name of Jesus, I bind the powers of hell!"

I would like to say that, at this moment, the devil fled and there were no further delays, but sometimes the battle does not end so quickly. Dawit did arrive at the family's home, but the sun was already up as he entered the house.

And Hayat had died several hours earlier.

Dawit entered the small house to find it jam packed with neighbors, friends, and family. He was not surprised by the crowd, however, because he had heard the wailing before he even got off his bike. With some difficulty, he pushed his way inside and saw a woman huddled in a corner, trembling with sobs, a scarf pulled tightly around her face, and Dawit knew it must be Tawbah. Her husband was trying to console her, but his own grief made his efforts futile.

Dawit squeezed through the crowd of mourners, all weeping and wailing, and moved into a small adjoining room. There lay little Hayat, covered with a sheet atop a table that a neighbor had lent the family. He knelt beside the body and laid his hand on her forehead, but it was already cold. Without further thought, he began praying.

"God, I asked you to be here before me!" He began to weep. "Please! Raise this little girl from the dead."

Friends and neighbors began to filter into the room, and soon a crowd had gathered around the stranger who knelt beside their beloved Hayat. Dawit ignored them and kept praying, but his body began to shake uncontrollably. "What is he doing?" whispered several. "Why pray for someone who is already dead?"

In Africa, death is a regular part of life. There are no funeral parlors in rural villages, no undertakers to quietly whisk away a dead relative and prepare the body for the funeral. Ordinary people are forced to deal with such traumatic times themselves, and Hayat's family had lovingly washed her dead body and folded her arms, waiting for her final burial garments. She was not in a swoon; she was not in a coma; she was dead. Tawbah's brother and nephews were already busy digging the grave. The girl was dead; the time for prayer was past.

But Dawit had learned that the time for prayer is never past, and he continued with trembling and tears. "Lord, many of these people do not know you. They are watching. Do not let me be ashamed, Father; let your name be glorified. Raise this girl from the dead!"

What was that? Dawit moved his hand from the girl's forehead to her cheek. Could there be warmth? He leaned closer and began to blow his breath on her face. Nothing happened; Dawit prayed on. Yes . . . there was warmth! Or was it just the heat of his own hand? Then motion—the girl's chest began to heave. She was breathing!

Suddenly, every noise stopped. The weeping, the wailing, the talking, the rustling—no sound, as everyone in the house held their breath.

Then Hayat opened her eyes. There was a collective gasp, but nothing more, as the mourners were too stunned to speak. Hayat lay on her back, rolling her eyes about the room, looking as puzzled and out of sorts as one who wakes from a powerful dream.

Dawit broke the silence. "Hayat?" he said, overwhelmed by what was happening.

"Yes?" The girl's voice was weak but very real.

And with that one word, the household burst into joyful shouts. Tawbah by this time had forced her way to her daughter's side, and she now threw herself full length atop the little table. The crowd around them wept and sang and danced, while those who could not fit inside the room ran outdoors to shout to anyone who would listen: "She is alive! She is alive!"

Poor Hayat was bewildered by the confusion, and she gripped her mother in a tight embrace. "Momma," she whispered, "where are my clothes?"

Here is what Hayat tells of her experience in the presence of God:

> I began to feel nauseous and weak in the afternoon, then I collapsed two times. . . . [She had suffered successive

convulsions, something she'd never experienced before or since.] Then, some time later, my soul was lifted up to heaven.

All was bright light around me, but there was a darker place nearby. In that darker area were people, lying on the ground. I didn't look at them much, because suddenly I saw Jesus, lifted up above me with a shining light coming from Him, and His light filled the air. He stood above, but a waterfall poured out from beneath His feet, poured down onto the people lying in darkness. White water flowed and sprayed everywhere, so the air was filled with brilliance like a rainbow.

Then I heard voices coming from the people who were lying nearby. "Don't let her go," they shouted. "Don't take her! Don't make her go!" Then Jesus spoke.

"Her time is not yet come," He said. "I am not bringing her home today. She is going to return and proclaim my name."

I did not understand all these things, but I could not take my eyes off Jesus. Then He turned to me and said, "There are two churches in your town. Go to them. Tell them that they must repent."

Then I saw a vision, like a picture on a screen behind Jesus, and it showed me an old building that was all dark and cold. Then light shone all around it, and the building began to glow, like it was coming alive, and grass around it became green, and everything came to life.

And Jesus said, "This is what I want you to do. Go and tell the churches that they must repent in my name, and I will bring them to life."

Hayat is a very shy, quiet girl, small for her age and very slender. She doesn't say much, as a general rule, and when she speaks it is with a very soft voice. But in the months that followed her resurrection, her family noticed a significant change in her life: she became very bold at certain times, accosting complete strangers in the street when the Spirit of God moved her. She was, not surprisingly, a sort of celebrity in the area, as word had spread far and wide of her resurrection. When God moved her spirit, she would approach someone, pull on his or her sleeve, and say, "I have a message for you from God. He has shown me some things you are doing, and He wants you to repent. He wants you to ask Jesus to forgive your sins, so He can raise you from the dead too!"

Now, there was a man who was present on the day she died, an imam who was friendly with her father. (Both Tawbah and Ubaid had told their friends about Jesus, and held a Bible study in their home, but prior to Hayat's death they had seen little fruit in their Muslim community.) This man's name was Wakil, and he had grown up in a strongly Muslim household. His father had committed him to become a sheikh one day, and from an early age he had been schooled at the dawah (Islamic school) in the Qur'an and other sacred Muslim writings. By his teen years, he was helping to teach at the local dawah, and he'd risen to be an imam at the local mosque, as well as to be a regular dawah instructor.

He also spent a good deal of time seeking out Christians to debate with, and that is how he had become friends with Hayat's parents. "You say that your Jesus is God," he would argue. "How can a man be God? Allah is one! The Qur'an also teaches that Isa was a prophet, but even a prophet cannot be God. There is only one God, and it is Allah; Allah has no son."

Yet, despite his obstinate rejection of Christ, Wakil considered Ubaid and Tawbah to be close friends. They had never become angry or defensive when he challenged their faith in Jesus; in fact, it was always Wakil who brought up the discussions in the first place. The couple would smile and answer his questions, yet they always invited him for coffee and for meals (Wakil was unmarried at the time), and seemed to look for ways they could help him. The couple had gone so far as to make him feel a part of their growing family, free to show up unannounced (usually around dinner time), welcome to stay late into the evening discussing politics and Christianity.

It was for this reason that Wakil had come quickly when he first learned of Hayat's seizures, and he had accompanied them silently on their visit to the clinic, carrying Hayat on his back on the return trip. He'd stayed in the home throughout the evening, sitting unnoticed as the girl's life ebbed away, and helping to prepare her body when she died. He had held the washbowl as Tawbah washed Hayat's lifeless body; had set out the clothing for her burial; had quietly wept while squeezing the girl's cold hand. He knew she was truly dead.

And he had stood dumbfounded when she came back to life.

"I have never heard of such a thing!" he thought, as he watched Hayat hugging her mother. "There is no such thing in the Qur'an." He'd gone outside where he could think more clearly, walking away from the cluster of friends and family. "If their Jesus can raise the dead, then He must be much more than just a prophet."

He didn't sleep much that night, as his mind continued to wrestle with this conundrum. From childhood, he had been taught—indeed, he had taught it himself for years—that Isa al Masih is merely another prophet from God, the twenty-fourth in succession, and that Christians are trying to create another god besides Allah when they claim that their Jesus is the Son of God. But no mere man can raise the dead back to life, so clearly something was not right in what he'd always believed.

The next morning, Wakil returned to Hayat's home, partly because he wanted to check on her parents after their ordeal, but also partly to see if Hayat was still alive. "Perhaps she just woke up briefly before dying," he tried to tell himself. But such reasonings brought no satisfaction because he knew without doubt that she was already dead when he helped prepare her body for burial. What he refused to admit to himself was that he wanted to know more about Jesus, to understand more clearly how to resolve this mystery.

As he walked through the door, there sat Hayat eating breakfast. She looked up at him, and her face glowed with joy. "Uncle Wahkee," she exclaimed (this was her childish pronunciation of his name). "Uncle Wahkee, I was praying that you would come today!" She leaped up and ran to give him a hug.

Wakil, somewhat taken aback, tried to make a joke. "You are very lively today for being dead yesterday," he said with a forced smile.

"It was only my body that was dead," she said, looking up to his face. Her eyes had a quality Wakil had not noticed before, as though she were suddenly wise beyond her years. "My spirit was not dead. I was with Jesus, and I felt more alive yesterday than I even do today."

"Tell me about Jesus." Wakil was stunned the moment the words left his lips, yet it was like opening a dam, and suddenly his hunger for the truth came flooding out. "How can God be a man? How can a prophet raise the dead? I need to understand these things! Tell me what you saw."

Hayat patiently described her experience in the presence of Jesus, but then she added something else. "Jesus gave me a message just for you, Uncle Wahkee. He said: 'Tell him that he must obey me and follow my Word. He must accept my salvation—then I will give my salvation to many others through him. He will lead many Muslims to me.' That is just what Jesus said; I memorized it!"

Today, Wakil will tell you, "I was immediately able to believe in Jesus, that He's the Lord and King, because I have seen it with my own eyes." He faced many challenges beginning that day, when word spread quickly that "the dawah imam" had suddenly become a Christian. "How can a persecutor of Christians suddenly *become* one?" people asked incredulously. His family quickly turned against him and tried to force him to move away, and one Muslim man tried to murder him with a spear. But we don't have time to tell his story, for we need to leave the continent of Africa to see how God is working in other areas of the world.

OBEDIENCE-BASED DISCIPLE MAKING

Jesus answered and said to him, "If anyone loves
Me, he will keep My word; and My Father will love
him, and We will come to him and make Our home
with him. He who does not love Me does not keep
My words; and the word which you hear is not Mine
but the Father's who sent Me." (John 14:23–24)

Jesus makes it very clear: if we love Him, we must obey
Him. This may sound like a strange teaching, but it's
only because we don't hear it very often. The converse
is also true: if we don't obey Him, then we don't love
Him. How can we be making real disciples if we don't
teach them to obey Jesus?

A year or so before Hayat's resurrection, Dave and Lynn Hunt
had moved back to the United States, called by Cityteam to
carry their discipling and church-planting work to California.
Little Salam, their adopted son, had grown strong and healthy,
and was as inquisitive and mischievous as any other infant. The
Hunts still referred to him sometimes as "our Baby of Peace,"
and in an indirect way, through his own example, he was to

provide a bridge for the gospel into yet another community by helping others to understand Jesus' way of making disciples.

And one of the people who needed to understand this lesson was me, Pat Robertson. Cityteam had begun its work as a rescue mission, offering both physical and spiritual healing to men and women struggling with such issues as alcohol and drug addiction. But the Lord had been leading the ministry to do much more than this, spreading the gospel through a wider ministry of making disciples in the ways that Jesus taught. We had learned of the miraculous things that were happening in distant lands, and the stories in this book are only a small glimpse of what God is doing worldwide. We wanted to understand why those things were happening overseas but not in the United States. I sat down for a long conversation with Dave the moment his family arrived in California.

"We've been hearing about great miracles, dreams and visions, healings, resurrections," I said. "Can those things happen here?"

"Of course they can!" Dave responded. "These miraculous things are by the Holy Spirit's hand, and He can do whatever He chooses wherever He chooses to do it." Dave looked thoughtful for a moment. "I think the fundamental issue is simply obedience to God's Word. When Christians follow the Lord's teachings on making disciples in all the world, we make ourselves available to the Holy Spirit to work."

I must confess that I bristled a bit at this comment. "We obey God's Word!" I said defensively. "We're trying to plant new churches and make converts—"

"That's part of the problem," Dave interrupted. "Jesus did not call us to 'make converts.' He said, 'Go therefore and *make disciples* of all the nations.'[18] There's a difference." I asked him to explain. "When we set out to make converts," he said, "our goal is to get a person to pray the 'sinner's prayer' or to make some statement of faith—but our goal needs to go way beyond that. We must train people how to obey the Word of God. That's what Jesus meant when He commanded the disciples to be 'teaching them to observe all things that I have commanded you.' We begin by teaching people to obey the Scriptures first. Then, when they come to understand what it means to be saved through the sacrifice of Jesus Christ, they already have developed the habit of obeying the Bible. When this happens, we have found that the new Christ follower soon discovers that Jesus also commanded the disciples to be baptized 'in the name of the Father and of the Son and of the Holy Spirit.' The first priority, however, is to make disciples."

Initially, Dave's ideas sounded radical to me. It seemed almost backward to suggest that a person should be taught to read the Bible before being taught what it means to be a Christian, but the more we talked and studied and prayed together, the more I came to realize that his ideas were not "his ideas" at all—they were the practical application of the teachings of Jesus. Dave asked me, "When Jesus sent out His disciples and told them to go and 'make disciples of all the nations,' was He sending them to people already converted, or was He sending them to the 'lost sheep'? We make disciples of the lost, Pat—not the saved!"

Dave used the metaphor of DNA to explain the basic concepts of becoming a disciple of Christ. "When you teach people how to *obey* Jesus," he said, "they will automatically begin doing it when they come to *know* Jesus. You're helping them shape a godly character in advance, helping to produce the DNA of godliness that grows into Christlike character once they become followers of Christ. But the DNA precedes the new birth." To understand these concepts, let's return to our story, picking up just prior to when Dave and Lynn returned to the States.

Emilia had grown up in a small town in Mexico. Her husband had abandoned her, and she had brought her six children to the United States in hopes of building a new life. She was working two full-time jobs and looking after six grandchildren when her eighteen-year-old daughter Rosalyn was diagnosed with Lupus. Suddenly, Emilia's hopes for an independent life were dashed, as her two paychecks were eaten up by medical bills; it wasn't long before the family was evicted from their small apartment. Emilia found herself huddling at night under a tree, together with six grandchildren and two children, using old blankets as a make-shift tent. She had come to America expecting a better life, but her family was worse off than they'd been in Mexico.

Emilia had attended the Catholic Church for many years, but her understanding of God was nominal at best. "I knew about God," she later explained, "but I had no conviction. I 'did church' because that's what it meant to be a Christian, I thought—and that was as far as it went." But each night she would listen to Rosalyn struggling to breathe, comforting the little ones as best she could, and she grew desperate.

One night, as rain dripped through the blankets, her spirit broke. "God," she cried out, "if you are real, please save my daughter! That is all I ask: heal Rosalyn. If you will make her well, I will serve you for the rest of my life."

Now, the tree where the family was huddling was near a small duplex apartment where a church met, and the next morning Emilia gathered her courage and knocked on one of the doors. It was opened immediately by Eduardo, a young man who worked for Cityteam, leading Discovery Bible Studies among the Spanish-speaking population of the area. As he listened to Emilia's tearful story, he realized that their meeting was no coincidence; he set to work getting Rosalyn admitted to a hospital and settling the family into genuine shelter.

Eduardo informally adopted Emilia's family as his own, spending countless hours with Rosalyn at the hospital and looking after the children when Emilia was working. He helped the family through the necessary steps to make their presence legal in the States; then he helped them secure medical insurance to cover Rosalyn's expenses. But more than these things, he began to pray. "And as soon as Eduardo began to pray," Emilia tells us, "Rosalyn began to get better." Her inflamed kidneys improved immediately, and Rosalyn began to breathe more freely. "That very day, I realized that God is real, and He was answering our prayers. I hadn't been following His Word, but that was the beginning of a dramatic transformation in my life."

Emilia began attending one of Eduardo's Discovery Bible Studies (DBS), and she quickly understood that God's Word was given to her so that she could obey it. Within a few months, she discovered Jesus' command that His disciples should be baptized, and she did so without further delay. It was around this time that Dave and Lynn returned to the States, and Dave had begun a series of training sessions, teaching Cityteam personnel and others how to disciple people to Christ. Eduardo had seen that Emilia was eager to share her new faith with others, so he invited her to attend. She had already learned from experience the importance of studying and obeying God's Word, but she took to heart two other important principles of discipleship: serving others by meeting their needs, and finding a person of peace. Emilia began praying intensely about the neighborhood where she now lived, asking God to lead her to someone whom He had already been preparing to hear the gospel.

One morning while she was praying, the Holy Spirit gave her a conviction to go to a certain street across town. She was scheduled to lead a DBS at noon, but this day she borrowed a van from Cityteam and took a detour across town to visit that street—all the way praying that God would show her what to do when she got there. She drove slowly along the street, wondering if God would send some dramatic sign—but the only sign she saw was a stop sign at a four-way intersection. An older woman was standing at the corner, however, waiting to cross the street, and their eyes met. And *that* was the sign Emilia was looking for.

"Hello!" she called with a big grin.

"Hello," the woman responded shyly.

"How are you doing today?"

"Fine, thanks." The woman seemed hesitant whether or not she should risk crossing the street in front of this odd stranger.

"What a beautiful day God has given us," Emilia pursued.

"Yes." The conversation did not seem promising, but suddenly the other woman became curious. "What are you doing in this neighborhood?" she asked. She had lived there most of her life, and evidently knew that Emilia was not a resident.

"I'm on my way to Bible study."

At this, the woman's face lit up. "Oh?" she said, stepping off the curb. "You teach Bible study?"

"Well, I don't teach a Bible study exactly; I teach people how to study the Bible for themselves and discover God."

The other woman was standing by her door now. "Please," she said, "can you park your car a minute?" And that began a lengthy conversation, as the other woman (whose name was Lorraine) began to pour out her questions and frustrations.

"I have been to many churches in my life," Lorraine said at one point, "but I still feel empty. I feel like there is a hole in my life someplace, but church does not mend it."

"This is different," Emilia responded. "The God that I know is the *real* God, and He will fill that empty place."

The two women were sitting in the van by this time, and Lorraine looked thoughtfully out the window for a moment. Then she turned to face her new friend with a look of determination. "Then I want to learn how to study the Bible and discover God. Please come to my house and teach me and my husband."

Emilia was overjoyed at this dramatic answer to her prayer, but God was not done yet. The following morning, she went to a grocery store and picked up a few items so she wouldn't arrive at Lorraine's home empty-handed: some instant coffee, a few cupcakes, enough snacks for four people. (She had also been trying to interest her own sister in attending Bible study, and this seemed like a perfect opportunity to take her along, since it would be a small group and her sister would not be intimidated.) That evening, Emilia and her sister drove to the apartment, and her sister went inside while Emilia parked the van. Before she was parked, however, her sister came running back, a look of alarm on her face.

"There's fifty people in there!" she cried. "Is this the right house?"

What Emilia hadn't known was that Lorraine and her husband had married young, many years earlier, and they'd been very busy ever since. They had nineteen children, eighteen grandchildren, and two great-grandchildren—and they had all come for the study, many bringing their spouses!

That evening, Emilia explained that the Bible is God's Word, and that God gave it to us so that we could know how to have eternal life through His Son, Jesus Christ. She found that the family owned Bibles and occasionally attended church, but they had never sat down to read it for themselves. The entire group, spanning all ages, was eager to learn more; and thus the Lord gave Emilia not one Bible study group to begin, but six! (She wisely determined right away that fifty people were too many for an effective study, and asked some of the siblings to host studies in their own homes.)

And this was just the beginning of a new ministry for this obedient follower of Christ. Emilia began to pray that God would show her how to teach more people to study the Bible, leading others to an understanding of God's grace as she had discovered with Eduardo. This was in September, when her grandchildren were beginning to attend school for the first time in their lives, and a woman at Family Services, a Cityteam compassion ministry, had given Emilia three backpacks for them to carry books and school supplies. She explained to Family Services that she wanted to serve some of the poorer neighborhoods in the area, and immediately received twenty backpacks to distribute to those who needed them.

In the coming months, Emilia began to knock on doors in that area, asking the residents if they had children who needed backpacks for school. The very first door was answered by a woman who had no children.

"Why are you giving away backpacks?" she asked. Emilia explained that she wanted to serve God by serving others, just as others had done for her.

"How does it serve God to give someone a backpack?" the woman persisted.

"If I meet a need in people's lives," Emilia explained, "I am showing them a little bit of God's love."

"And what difference does that make?"

"Well, some people might want to know more about God. Then I offer to teach them how to study God's book and discover God. If they're not interested, that's okay; someone else will be."

"I'd like to study God's book," the woman said instantly. "What's the name of it?"

Three days later, Emilia returned to the woman's home to teach her how to study the Bible, expecting to meet with her and her husband. When she arrived, she could hardly get inside because there were so many people present. The woman had called all her friends and family, inviting them to come learn how to study the Bible, and nearly forty-five people had shown up! On the night of the second study, the group had grown in numbers rather than diminished, and halfway through, a housing inspector came and told them that they were violating the city's fire codes. This forced Emilia once again to break the group into smaller Bible studies that met in different homes around the city. Those groups grew and spawned new Bible studies, which in turn put down roots as home churches, and it wasn't long before there were small churches being planted that were in the second and third generation of church growth.

One of these "splinter groups" that started from that home Bible study was led by a woman named Juanita. She also had emigrated from Mexico, where she had been involved in a small Bible study years earlier. I had the opportunity to talk with her during this time, and she told me that her group was currently reading from Genesis 22, where Abraham was called to sacrifice Isaac on the altar. I asked her what pictures she saw there of the sacrifice of Christ on the cross, and she responded with a blank look. "No," she said after a moment, "this is about Abraham, not Jesus."

I realized that her group had not yet gotten to the New Testament, as they were following the DBS reading plan outlined by Cityteam,[19] and she did not yet understand how Abraham's willing sacrifice provided a prophetic picture of God's gift of His Son on the cross. I must confess that I was a little troubled at the time, wondering how a group of non-Christians could be learning about Jesus when they were being taught by someone who didn't even understand it herself. But what I didn't recognize at the time was that Juanita and her fellow students were developing an important spiritual DNA, learning to respect the Bible as God's Word, laying a foundation for a deeper understanding of who Jesus is. This is why we call the process *Discovery* Bible Study: because the Holy Spirit enables a person to discover the truth about Christ through the pages of Scripture.

If you ask Juanita today to explain how Abraham and Isaac pictured Christ, she will explain the deeper significance of Genesis 22 in terms that would satisfy any theologian. In fact, she now volunteers with Cityteam training people in the process of discipling others to obey God's Word, and she lives out those principles herself as a committed follower of Christ. But this transformation was the work of the Holy Spirit, teaching Juanita and many others about Jesus through His Word—it was not the result of any manmade program or ministry scheme.

Dave Hunt refers to this process as "counterintuitive," encouraging people who know nothing of Jesus to begin leading a Bible study in their own homes. "Shouldn't we ensure that mature Christians are the ones teaching Scripture?" I'd asked him years ago, but his response surprised me. "How can it be a bad thing," he said, "to encourage someone to study the Bible? We tend to forget the role of the Holy Spirit in the process of being born again. Without the Holy Spirit's intervention, no one could be saved. Our job is to lead others to God's Word, then let the Spirit teach what it means."

This, of course, does not mean that deliberate discipleship is not important. We at Cityteam train Christ followers how to grow in faith and obedience, but all our training is based solely upon the Scriptures. It is vitally important, therefore, that people understand right from the beginning that Jesus is the source of all truth, and that truth is found in His Word. A habit of going to the Bible for answers produces the necessary DNA for a person to grow into a committed follower of Christ.

The experiences of Regina and Raul will illustrate this.

14

PERSON OF PEACE

> But whatever house you enter, first say, "Peace to this house." And if a son of peace is there, your peace will rest on it; if not, it will return to you. And remain in the same house, eating and drinking such things as they give, for the laborer is worthy of his wages. Do not go from house to house. . . . But whatever city you enter, and they do not receive you, go out into its streets and say, "The very dust of your city which clings to us we wipe off against you. Nevertheless know this, that the kingdom of God has come near you." (Luke 10:5–7, 10–11)

The "person of peace" principle that Jesus taught was so important that, if the disciples could not discover a person of peace, they were to move on, dust off their sandals, and leave! When you enter a new community, you are viewed as an outsider, and people will naturally be suspicious. The insider knows the community and has a close circle of friends; they trust each other, but they don't trust you. Finding a person of peace can remove this barrier, as that person brings you into his or her close circle of friends and family, opening many new doors for the Word of God.

By the time Raul turned fifty, he had experimented with just about everything the world has to offer. He had once been a successful businessman in Argentina who owned and managed restaurants, but that seemed like the distant past. He was now just a hardened man who had lived a hard life, and the only thing he had to show for it was a hard heart. He was a heavy drinker, was addicted to cocaine, and habitually lost whatever money he earned by gambling. Around Christmas one year, he hit rock bottom. With no money, no job, no home, and no hope, he started walking in search of a way to kill himself. What he found instead was the Source of Life, for he unexpectedly came upon one of Cityteam's recovery shelters in the Tenderloin district, the "Skid Row" of San Francisco. And for lack of a better idea, he went inside.

"Some guy came over to me," Raul laughs about today, "and greeted me like I was a long lost brother. He was just a little guy, but full of God's love; you could just feel it! I was a total mess, but this guy loved me—and what a huge impact that had on my life!" Over the course of the following year, Raul was discipled by that man, who worked with Cityteam, and in the process he learned the importance of studying and obeying the Scriptures.

At that time, Cityteam was conducting Bible studies in which a Christian would teach and lecture on what the Scriptures mean. We had not yet begun the Discovery Bible Study process in which each person is called upon to study the

Word for himself, allowing the Holy Spirit the "breathing room" to illuminate the student as He sees fit. Nevertheless, Raul had reached the point where he recognized that he needed salvation through the sacrifice of Christ, and he grew in his faith by leaps and bounds. The Holy Spirit gave him release from his addictions, and he quickly understood that the Bible is intended not merely to be studied, but to be obeyed and applied.

Meanwhile, one of Cityteam's community outreach coordinators, a woman named Betty, had been facing some communication barriers in the Hispanic community, and she eventually asked Raul for help, since he was fluent in Spanish and English. Her initial intention was to have Raul act as a translator in her efforts to teach the Scriptures, but it was at this time that Dave and Lynn Hunt helped to redirect Cityteam's focus on spreading the gospel. One of the issues that the Hunts pointed out was that Cityteam was doing well in finding "access ministries" to reach people—meeting human needs by giving away backpacks and food boxes or teaching English as a second language (ESL) classes—but we were not following Jesus' command to seek out a person of peace to act as a bridge into a larger community, and we were not allowing people to discover God's love for themselves by the power of the Holy Spirit and the Word of God.

It was Raul who put that command into practice. Betty and others had been visiting a certain community and doing prayer walking[20] almost every weekend for two years, but Betty had begun to get disheartened about something happening in the very hard and poor neighborhood. Raul and Betty went there to deliver food boxes to the inhabitants of the rundown apartments. In the process, they met a woman who gladly accepted the food boxes, but remained quite reserved in her conversation with Betty and Raul. Her name was Regina.

Now Regina had actually met some other Cityteam people in the past, and they had invited her to join a Bible study. She had been polite, but remained firmly resistant to any study commitment. Betty knew this, and gave Raul the woman's phone number, asking him to make a follow-up call to see if there was anything else they could do to help her. Raul phoned her immediately.

"I'd like to teach you how to study the Bible," he told her.

"I'd like to study the Bible," she responded, "but frankly, I don't trust you."

This statement took Raul aback, but as he gently pursued the issue he learned that a number of Christians over the years, including some of the Cityteam workers, had promised Regina that they would help her understand the Word of God, but for one reason or another had never followed up on their promise.

"Listen," Raul said earnestly, "Jesus is the only answer to all of life's struggles, and the only way to understand Jesus is to study His book and do what it says. I know this, because God showed me how to put my life back together through obedience to the book. I want to help you that way too."

"No, *you* listen," she said, softly but very firmly. "I don't have time for people who don't do what they promise. I want to obey God, but I don't want to waste my time with you."

Then the Spirit of God moved through Raul. "I solemnly promise you: if I say I'll teach you the Bible, I will do so. I *will* keep my word!" For reasons she could not explain at the time, Regina softened at those words, and with some trepidation agreed to meet with Raul.

And, needless to say, Raul kept his word. Regina had been divorced for many years, and was living in a small apartment with her six grandchildren. Her four children were all grown with families of their own, twelve grandchildren in all; her two daughters worked full-time, and their children spent most of their time with Regina. So Raul had a ready-made small group for Bible study, as the youngsters would gather at the dining room table to listen to stories about heroes like King David and Daniel in the lions' den. Raul did the things that Betty and Dave had taught him, and soon Regina was facilitating the Discovery Bible Study, while he assumed the role of coach, participating in the group but letting Regina lead. And over the following months, that small group grew to include some twenty adults, mostly friends and neighbors of Regina.

But something else grew during that time as well—something quite unexpected: Regina and Raul fell in love. Ordinarily, a disciple maker like Raul will help a person of peace begin a Discovery Bible Study, teaching him or her what it means to be a disciple of Christ, obeying God's teachings of Scripture. But soon after the study is established, the discipler turns the study over to the person of peace, moving on to find another person of peace to start the process over again. This prevents the disciple maker from becoming the "authority figure" in the group by switching instead to a coaching role, allowing God to work as He wills in the lives of those studying His Word.

On this occasion, however, it would have been difficult for Raul to leave the study, because within the year the couple was married. Nevertheless, Regina quickly understood and embraced the disciple-making concepts Jesus taught in the New Testament, and it wasn't long before she was working alongside her new husband, seeking out persons of peace and sharing the gospel.

The process of finding a person of peace is sometimes very straightforward and simple. A follower of Christ meets someone who does not know Christ, yet who shows an openness and interest in learning about Him and studying His Word. This generally demonstrates that God has already been at work in that person's life, preparing him or her to hear the message of salvation. Yet that is not always so readily obvious, as we have already seen in many chapters of this book. One such example was Nora.

Regina met Nora one afternoon at the local union hall, as both women were looking for work. They struck up a conversation and were pleased to discover that they both had emigrated to the United States from Nicaragua during the years following the Communist overthrow of Nicaragua's government by the Sandinistas. (In 1989, the Sandinistas murdered Regina's brother, and she fled to the US to escape.) Regina gradually turned the conversation to the things of God, but she was met with a sudden hostility from her new friend. Nora let her know, in no uncertain terms, that she'd had some unpleasant experiences in the past with people calling themselves Christians, and she wanted nothing to do with Regina's Bible studies.

Despite this disappointment, Regina invited Nora to join her for lunch that day, and a friendship developed between them. They would meet several times each week at the union hall, and that grew into frequent visits at one another's homes, which grew into Nora stopping by for dinner with Regina and Raul once or twice a week. Regina did not try to broach the topic of God's Word any further after Nora's initial rebuke, yet she continued to be a good friend and a sympathetic ear.

Then one week, quite unexpectedly, Nora arrived at Regina's house just as their Discovery Bible Study was beginning.

"Oh," said Nora, "you have some friends here tonight?"

"We're just about to sit down for Bible study," Regina answered in a nonchalant fashion. Nora knew full well that they held Bible studies on Wednesday evenings, but Regina did not allude to that.

"Well, don't let me stop you," Nora said as she settled herself into an armchair in the living room. The couple's home features a large room, part living room and part dining area, and the Bible study group would crowd around the large dining table at one end. Nora sat at the far end of the room and turned up the volume on the television.

This was the beginning of a regular pattern, as Nora would "coincidentally" stop by the couple's home every Wednesday evening, just as Bible study was about to commence. Regina never commented on the timing, nor did she urge her friend to join them. She would have some popcorn all ready, the TV remote control handy by the armchair, and Nora would settle in to watching her favorite programs without more than a hello. The second or third time this happened, Raul raised an objection to his wife in private.

"She turns up the volume to drown us out," he said in exasperation. "We're just encouraging her to disrupt our Bible study!"

Regina nodded in agreement, but then added thoughtfully, "But at least she's here. We can still do our study—we just need to talk a little louder."

Raul was not convinced. "I'm afraid that some of us find it a distraction. I know I do. We need to provide an environment that's conducive to studying God's Word."

"I agree," Regina answered, "but God has brought her here to us. Don't you think we should let Him do His work?"

Raul finally saw the wisdom in his wife's gentle urging, and the couple began to pray intently that God would change Nora's heart. It did not happen immediately, but God's answer did come. One night, after about two months of the loud TV, Nora left her armchair and came to the dining table.

"I'm out of popcorn," she announced without preamble.

Regina looked up from her Bible. "There's the kitchen," she answered with a smile. Nora was not offended by the pointed response, but her next move surprised the dozen or so people gathered at the table. She picked up an empty chair from nearby, set it down in the kitchen doorway facing away from the dining room, then knelt herself down on it—facing backward and staring at the people gathered to study God's Word. She did not say anything further, but she also did not make any more popcorn. She simply sat backward on that chair and watched as the study continued. When the study ended, Nora immediately rose from the chair and left without a word.

The next week, Nora forsook the television altogether, hovering in the kitchen until the study started. She then took the same chair, positioned it the same way, and repeated the previous week's silent observation. The people around the table found this somewhat disconcerting, perhaps even more distracting than a loud TV, but they had all been praying every week for their strange guest, so they made the best of the situation. And Nora repeated the performance the following week.

About halfway through that study, however, something happened. The group had been studying Genesis, and someone raised a question about what constituted a "day" in the passage. They were wrestling with the question of when a day begins in God's timetable, when suddenly a strange voice was heard.

"A day starts at midnight."

Every head around the table started up, and wondering eyes turned toward the kitchen. There sat Nora, looking as though she had merely stated an obvious fact. There was a moment of uncertain silence, then Regina started to laugh.

"Okay," she said, walking toward her friend with open arms, "I think it's time for you to come sit at the table now."

Since that time, Nora has become a committed follower of Christ, and she is one of the most active participants each week in Regina and Raul's Discovery Bible Study. But when Regina first met her, she immediately assumed that Nora was not a person of peace; indeed, she was openly hostile to Christianity. Yet we can never assume that we know what God is doing in the life of another person, and there are times when He leads His followers into unexpected relationships specifically because He has a miraculous plan to unfold. And He was busy at that time unfolding yet another such plan for Raul and Regina.

One of Regina's children was Alonzo, an outgoing young man of twenty-five. He had been just a little boy when his uncle was murdered and his mother fled with him and his siblings to the United States, and he had a growing desire to revisit the places and people he had left behind. There was a period of shutdown at his job, so he took advantage of the time off to spend a couple months in Nicaragua. He reconnected with a group of friends in the town where he'd been born, spending his days exploring and his evenings joining in the activities of those young people. Back home, he did join with Regina and Raul in the

Bible studies, but he had not yet committed his life to be a follower of Christ. His intention on this trip was to have a relaxing vacation, not to spread the gospel to Nicaragua, but God had His own plans for his future.

And those plans included a young lady named Lily. She lived with her mother and sisters in the town where Alonzo was staying, attending school during the days and working most evenings as a housekeeper for families in town. It just so happened that Alonzo and his friends went to a party one evening when Lily wasn't working, and quite by coincidence, Lily went too. ("There are no 'coincidences,'" Lily's mother said to me recently. "God always has a purpose.") The two met and hit it off immediately, and Alonzo spent the next month getting to know Lily and her family. By the time he returned to the States, the young man was hopelessly in love. The two developed their relationship as best they could by e-mail and Internet and telephone, but at the end of a year Alonzo had decided that his life was incomplete without her. So he returned to Nicaragua, married Lily, lived with her and her family during another of his employer's six-week shutdown periods, then regretfully returned to his job in California—leaving behind a lonely wife with a baby in her womb.

And like little Salam, Dave Hunt's adopted child, that unborn daughter would become a bridge for the gospel into a whole new community.

HOW DISCIPLES ARE MADE

Now when they saw the boldness of Peter and John, and perceived that they were uneducated and untrained men, they marveled. And they realized that they had been with Jesus. And seeing the man who had been healed standing with them, they could say nothing against it. (Acts 4:13-14)

For you see your calling, brethren, that not many wise according to the flesh, not many mighty, not many noble, are called. But God has chosen the foolish things of the world to put to shame the wise, and God has chosen the weak things of the world to put to shame the things which are mighty; and the base things of the world and the things which are despised God has chosen, and the things which are not, to bring to nothing the things that are, that no flesh should glory in His presence. (1 Corinthians 1:26-29)

Jesus chose unschooled, ordinary people to do His work because, in that way, people would understand that what was happening could only be of God. Those who oppose can only stand in silence because the miracle is

unfolding before them. Join us in praising Him for what
He is doing!

———————————

Lily's parents, Lenora and Benito, lived in a mountainous area
of Nicaragua surrounded by volcanoes, some of which are
still active, where sugarcane is the dominant source of liveli-
hood. Benito was a laborer in the sugarcane fields, working
together with his friend Jorge and Jorge's two sons. Each day,
the men would go into the fields that surrounded their homes to
work at growing or harvesting the sugar, labor that was arduous
but rewarding. The men were content with their lot in life, and
would have willingly continued into later years, teaching their
grandsons to carry on after them.

But there was a problem with their occupation, a widespread
epidemic that is continuing even today in many parts of the
world: the danger of kidney disease. Countless men who work
the sugarcane in Nicaragua contract renal failure, a disease of
the kidneys that leads rapidly to death from internal infections.
The cause is not known; it might be connected with chemicals
used for fertilizers and pesticides, or it might be caused by long
hours of hard labor in the heat without adequate water intake.
Crop dusters fly over the fields on a regular basis to cover the
cane with various chemicals, and the cane is eventually set on
fire before harvesting to kill snakes and speed the labor. These
factors, combined with the dry, hot climate and hard work,
could all work together in some lethal fashion—and all these
things might be further exacerbated by widespread use of alcohol and painkillers. But whatever is causing the problem, the
results are devastating, as many thousands of men die each year
at an early age.

Benito began to show symptoms of this dreaded condition when he was around thirty years old. He would return home from the fields utterly exhausted, collapsing on his bed and not getting up again before dawn. He had trouble keeping food down, and would sometimes collapse in dizziness and nausea while working; on other occasions, he would be doubled over with cramps. He had always been a tall, burly man, but suddenly he slimmed down to such an extent that his clothes no longer fit, and his powerful muscles seemed to have atrophied. It wasn't long before he was unable to work in the sugar fields, leaving his family without any source of income.

Understandably, Benito felt frustrated and impotent in his weakened condition, and he could not escape the realization that his disease was likely to end in death. He began to think, for the first time in his life, about what role God played in the fates of men, and one Sunday morning he hobbled alone to a large church in the nearby town. It seemed like entering another world to this man of the soil, for he found himself surrounded by people of wealth and influence. He sat silently as the congregation sang songs he didn't know, and listened attentively to the woman who preached a sermon on topics that were strange to him. As his attention began to wander, he idly picked up a Bible from the pew and began to read at random.

That event changed his future, and the futures of his family and many other people. He had opened roughly to the middle of the book, and he read:

> Yea, though I walk through the valley of the shadow of death, I will fear no evil; for You are with me; Your rod and Your staff, they comfort me. You prepare a table before me in the presence of my enemies; You anoint my head with oil; my cup runs over. Surely goodness and mercy shall follow me

all the days of my life; and I will dwell in the house of the
LORD forever.[21]

From that day on, Benito developed a love for the Scriptures.
He spent long hours on his bed, reading more or less at random.
He did not always comprehend what he read; some of the stories seemed strange and beyond his own experience, while other
passages were so poetic or prophetic that he could only scratch
his head in wonder. But one thing remained consistent every
time he opened the book: he sensed that the words contained
eternal truth, and he grew in a conviction that somehow the
power of God was with him as he read.

Benito attended that church only a few more times, but
he never came to feel at home there. Walking the distance to
town was exceedingly taxing on his weakening legs, but he
also viewed the church as a sort of private club, an exclusive
membership where he would never fit in. (It is not our place to
speculate on the reasons for this; I merely state Benito's percep-
tions.) Yet he recognized almost instinctively that the things he
was reading were meant to be shared, not hoarded to oneself,
so he began to spend time every evening reading the Bible to
his wife and daughters. Lenora responded immediately to those
readings, and soon she had developed the habit of reading from
the Scriptures every morning as well.

In the course of time, Benito's condition grew grave, and he
was admitted to a hospital for treatment and tests. Benito was
on oxygen, and Lenora sat holding his hand as they saw a doctor
approaching with the results, her face very somber.

"Your GFR numbers are very high," she said, referring to
tests that revealed acute kidney failure. Then she leaned her
face close to Benito with a callous expression. "You should have

been in your coffin long ago!" Turning to Lenora, she added, "There is nothing we can do. He is on his way to die."

Lenora burst into tears and loud sobs, but her husband squeezed her hand. "You know where you need to go now," he said gently. "Read to me from Psalms."

The rest of that day, Lenora sat by her husband's side, reading from the Bible as he struggled to breathe. Then, in the early evening hours, he glanced at her significantly, and she knew that the time had come. Without even thinking, Lenora stood up, placed the Bible on her husband's chest, and prayed. "Receive him, Father," she cried out, "in the name of Jesus!"

Lenora had no theological training, no Sunday school upbringing, and she scarcely understood the nature of God's plan of salvation through the sacrifice of Christ on the cross. But she did understand that God is in control of all things, and she knew that Jesus was central to God's purposes in some way—her faith in these truths grown only out of reading the Bible together with her husband.

"I've always been in God's hands," she says today. "I asked God often in that time to heal my husband, to give me a testimony of His answering prayer that I could share with others. But that was not part of His plan."

During the weeks and months following Benito's death, Lenora grew increasingly angry and resentful toward God. "Why would God not heal my husband?" she asked herself daily. On one occasion, a friend was telling her about a young man who had been healed of kidney failure, and she interrupted the story with the cry, "But what about me? Where was *my* healing?" One night, not long after, Lenora had a dream.

She found herself standing outside her home, the door closed against her as she stood in the darkness of night. "I must get inside," she told herself, "for my husband's body must be buried." She opened the door and entered to find her home flooded with light. At the center of the main room there was a coffin, resting on two trestles or sawhorses, the lid open and her husband lying inside. She noticed, however, that his face was flushed with life, and as she stared he opened his eyes, sat up, stretched himself, and began to climb out.

"What are you doing, Benito?" she cried.

He looked at her with a joyful grin. "Doing?" he responded. "I'm going to the bathroom! You don't mind, do you?"

The incongruity made Lenora burst out in laughter, laughter that was more joy than simple mirth. Her parents, long since dead in reality, suddenly appeared in the room, also laughing, and she turned to them in question.

"My husband . . . he is *alive*!" Her parents merely laughed the more heartily. The main room was sectioned off from the bedrooms by a drapery of white linen, and Lenora thrust it aside to rush into the bedroom in search of her husband who had walked out. She could not see into that room for some reason, however, as though her eyes could not penetrate beyond the drapes. She turned back to the main room, and found things in a more mundane condition—the brilliance had left, her parents were not there, yet the coffin still remained. And inside it she saw her husband lying dead, as though nothing miraculous had transpired.

But then she noticed that Benito was not alone in the coffin. Beside his dead body there was another man seated, gazing calmly upon Benito's face as though he were merely sleeping.

"Who are you?" Lenora cried. When the man made no answer, she said, "What did you give to my husband?"

The man turned to Lenora. "I anointed him with oil," he said.

"Make him live again!" she cried, tears streaming down her cheeks.

"My daughter," the man said gently, "I already have."

"Then why is he *dead* again?" Lenora demanded, stamping her foot in anger.

"There is a healing for this world," he answered, "but there is another healing that brings eternal life. Which is more important to you?"

When Lenora awoke from this strange dream, she was puzzled at what it meant, but she understood the most important fact: that her husband had been given eternal life, and she would never trade that just to have him back in this life.

It was several years later that Lenora's daughter Lily married Alonzo. Alonzo had to continue living in the States to earn an income, while Lily and her baby daughter were living in Nicaragua with Lenora. To supplement Alonzo's regular financial support, Lenora found work caring for the elderly—work that was inconsistent and unpredictable, based upon the needs of any given patient—which frequently took her to live in distant areas. Eventually, increasingly high blood pressure caught up with her, and she was forced to retire and depend solely upon what Alonzo could provide. The future seemed bleak, but she had learned one important lesson from her continued habit of reading the Bible: the past cannot be changed; the future cannot be known; what matters is the present.

So Lenora filled her time in helping Lily with the baby, looking after the endless chores of running a household, and trying to share her love for the Bible with young people. And there seemed to be an endless supply of young people; for all of

Lily's friends and neighbors delighted in coming to the house to dote over her infant, gossip about their lives, and do all the things that young people do all over the world. Lenora would frequently chat with these friends, telling them about what she had read that morning in the Bible, sometimes sharing stories of laughter or tears about her late husband. Yet she felt a deep desire to do more, to have a clear purpose in teaching others about God—but she didn't know how.

Another complication arose from the basic responsibilities of life. Lenora was finding it increasingly difficult to keep pace with Lily and the baby, along with the many visits and activities of Lily's friends. Housework was demanding enough without the added burdens of what seemed like a growing, energetic family. Her high blood pressure was under control, but the medications sapped her of stamina.

One day, as she was hanging out some laundry, her friend Rita came past. Rita's husband Jorge, Benito's old friend and workmate, had since died of kidney failure, and her tragedy was multiplied several times over—for two of her sons had also died, and the third was in the advanced stages of the same disease. Soon there would be no one left of the group of friends who had once co-labored in the sugar fields. Lenora realized that she was not alone in this tragedy, and both words and tears came pouring forth.

"Rita! Come help us! We can't keep up with the burdens of life. Please come!"

From that day on, Lenora's family grew by one more, as Rita spent most of her waking hours helping them with cooking, cleaning, laundry, and the countless other daily tasks of life. She also joined Lenora in studying the Bible, and in offering counsel and guidance to the young women in their growing circle. She and Lenora also tried attending the church Benito had visited earlier, but they were disappointed to find that nobody seemed interested in studying the Bible with them. For both women, understanding and obeying the Scriptures was a top priority, but they longed for a deeper understanding.

And that was when Regina came to visit. She had often thought of returning to her native village in Nicaragua, but having a granddaughter that she'd never seen moved her desire into action. She made her arrangements, then phoned Lenora (whom she'd never met) to let her know her plans. Before hanging up, she added, "Oh, by the way—do you ever read the Bible?"

Lenora was startled but delighted by this *non sequitur*. "Why . . . yes," she stammered, "I love to read my Bible. Do you?"

"Oh, yes, it's the foundation of my life. In fact, I help lots of other people learn how to study it and obey God's design for our lives. I can teach you, too, if you'd like."

That visit began a new chapter in the lives of Lenora and Rita. Regina had spent a week traveling around Nicaragua, visiting family and old friends in various areas. When she arrived in Lenora's town, however, her top priority was to meet her new granddaughter—and to continue the conversation about Discovery Bible Study.

Regina is quiet and reserved by nature, but her friends and family had noticed an inexplicable change in her character since becoming a Christ follower: whenever the topic of Bible study came up, she would be transformed from shyness to a gifted speaker. "She is normally a very timid person," her husband, Raul, will tell you, "but when she starts talking about God, she has no problem. She can talk about the Bible for twenty-four hours!" I've seen this transformation myself. When the conversation turns to the things of God, the Holy Spirit simply fills this shy woman, transforming her into a prophetic witness for His glory.

And that topic seemed to come up in nearly every conversation on her trip to Nicaragua that summer. As Lenora observed, "Anyone and everyone she spoke to, she talked about Bible study!" The day of her arrival in town, Regina went straight to see Lenora.

"So," she said soon after introducing herself, "you'd like to lead a Bible study in your home?"

Lenora was a little taken aback, both by the sudden shift in conversation (Regina was already coddling her granddaughter), and by her visitor's presumption. "I didn't say I wanted to *teach* Bible study," she protested. "I want to *learn* about the Bible." After a moment, she added, "Maybe when I learn more, then I could think about teaching others."

Regina smiled without taking her eyes from the baby in her arms. "That is how you learn," she said, "by studying the Bible with others. You all learn and grow together. You're not a teacher with students; you're all students studying and learning to obey—together."

Rita was in the kitchen preparing lunch, and she called out, "That's a great idea! Let's do it, Lenora!" But Lenora was not persuaded. In contrast to Regina, she was naturally outgoing and gregarious, a woman who loved to entertain in her home, and it wasn't the notion of holding a study that she found daunting. There were two large problems looming in her mind: she barely had enough money to feed her family and wouldn't dream of inviting neighbors and friends without offering hospitality; even more significant, she simply did not feel qualified to answer difficult questions about God's Word, regardless of Regina's encouragement.

But Lenora's lack of enthusiasm did not quell that of Regina, and for the next week she told everyone she met about the new Bible study that would soon begin at Lenora's home. One such person was a man named Immanuel who operated a large tricycle taxi around town. He would sit on the tricycle seat above the front wheel, his passengers would occupy a bench seat between the two rear wheels, and he would pedal them wherever they wanted to go. Regina had hired him on her first day to take her to Lenora's house, since she didn't know where it was located, and almost immediately had begun to converse with him as though they'd been friends for years.

"You look thoughtful today," she said cheerfully as she settled onto the taxi seat.

Immanuel laughed self-consciously. "Oh, well . . . I guess I have a few things on my mind. Nothing serious, though," he added quickly, as he peddled into traffic.

"Whatever troubles us is serious in God's eyes," Regina persisted. "Do you read the Bible?"

Regina was not aggressive in her conversations—she never made a person feel condemned or inferior—but she was persistent. She sensed in her spirit that Immanuel was deeply troubled about something, and by the time they arrived at Lenora's house, she had learned that he was facing both financial and marital problems. "I will pray for you," she said earnestly as she paid her fare. "And I will need a ride home later, so please come back here at three o'clock." On her return trip that day, she resumed the conversation about the Bible, and she also asked Immanuel to pick her up first thing the next morning to take her shopping.

Over the course of the next two weeks, Regina rode in Immanuel's taxi every day. She frequently had to invent errands or visits to friends, but she always found a reason to spend time with him, talking about God's desire to answer prayer, and the truth just waiting to be discovered inside His Word. Immanuel never had any lunch or dinner with him, so Regina frequently stopped at a market on their trips together, putting together an impromptu meal for them to share. On such stops, of course, she would also start conversations with the market sellers, inevitably turning the topic to God's Word and His Son, Jesus Christ. And Immanuel was always standing nearby, silently listening.

One afternoon, Regina stopped for a visit with her grand-daughter, and Lenora met her at the door. "I had two people stop me yesterday," she said with some heat, "one I don't even know! They both said they're planning on coming to my Bible study!" She glared at Regina over the top of her glasses. "*What* Bible study?"

"Oh, don't let that bother you," Regina answered casually, heading straight for the crib. "If people come to the house, just offer them some coffee or juice, some cookies, then sit down and chat. God will help you with the rest."

Lenora's eyes welled up. "But I can't *afford* that!" she wept.

Regina rushed to embrace her. "Don't worry about that either," she said. "God will help you with *all* the details." The next day, she arrived at Lenora's house with a supply of coffee, fruit juices, and a variety of snacks. "This will get you started when people come for Bible study," she explained. "My husband and I will help you in the future to have enough food to share. Just obey God's Word, and He will take care of the details."

The day after Regina returned to the States, a man knocked on Lenora's door. "My name is Immanuel," he said, "and a woman named Regina said you were holding a Bible study here." Lenora was beginning to get used to this sort of encounter, and she invited the man inside for some coffee. "Oh, I hope I'm not too late for the Bible study," he answered hastily. "I need to understand the Bible. I need God's help in my life!" And suddenly Regina understood. "The Bible led me to the peace of God," she told herself, "so I should share that with this man."

Some time after this, Raul told me about Lenora and Rita—and he said that there were eighty new Discovery Bible Studies in three major cities of Nicaragua! When we heard the story, Cityteam quickly sent Betty there to find out if the stories were true. Betty returned saying, "No, it's *not* true that there are eighty new groups studying the Bible—there are *over a hundred*!" With that shocking news, I promptly sent Dave Hunt and others to Nicaragua to continue the training that Regina had started, showing the men and women how to lead Discovery Bible Studies—and I went with them to hear these stories firsthand and see what was happening with my own eyes. To our delight, we found that both Lenora and Rita have blossomed into full-fledged disciple makers for Christ. I had the privilege of sitting in on a training session as the two women taught more than fifty new disciples how to go out and begin leading their own Discovery Bible Studies.

And this is not the end of the story! Rita went back to her community in the middle of the sugarcane region and started her own Discovery Bible Studies. She cannot read, so she brings her eleven-year-old grandson along, and he reads the Scripture passage for that week's lesson. When I was there, Rita had started fifteen groups in several different villages, with more than three hundred people attending—most of them widows of kidney disease.

The Word of God is going forth in great power around the world, as ordinary people like Regina joyfully tell others about God's Word, and people like Lenora and Rita humbly obey what they learn. This is what Jesus intended disciple making to be like: a worldwide movement starting with a person of peace and a simple "discovery process" led by ordinary people reading God's Word. As they simply obey the simple truths God reveals to them, these ordinary people are being coached along and are growing in their faith and understanding of God's will for their lives.

This is how disciples are made!

NOTES

1. Sura 6:84–85.

2. Sura 3:3.

3. Sura 21:35.

4. See Sura 3:55.

5. Sura 19:33–34.

6. Acts 5:29.

7. See the first book in this series, *Miraculous Movements*, for more information on how Jesus commanded His disciples to share the gospel.

8. Sura 19:35.

9. Isaiah 52:14–15.

10. Isaiah 53:1–12.

11. Sura 4:171.

12. John 14:6; 3:3, 16.

13. *Herod* was a title like *Pharaoh* or *Caesar*, rather than a person's name; there were numerous Herods in the Bible.

14. Sura 19:12–15.

15. More of Ali's story can be found in another book in this series, *Miraculous Movements*.

16. Sura 3:55–56.

17. Sura:174–75.

18. Matthew 28:19–20.

19. See *Miraculous Movements*, which outlines this Bible study.

20. Prayer walking is the strategy of walking the streets of a neighborhood and praying explicitly for the residents in the homes, workers in the businesses, and people on the street as one goes along.

21. Psalm 23:4–6.